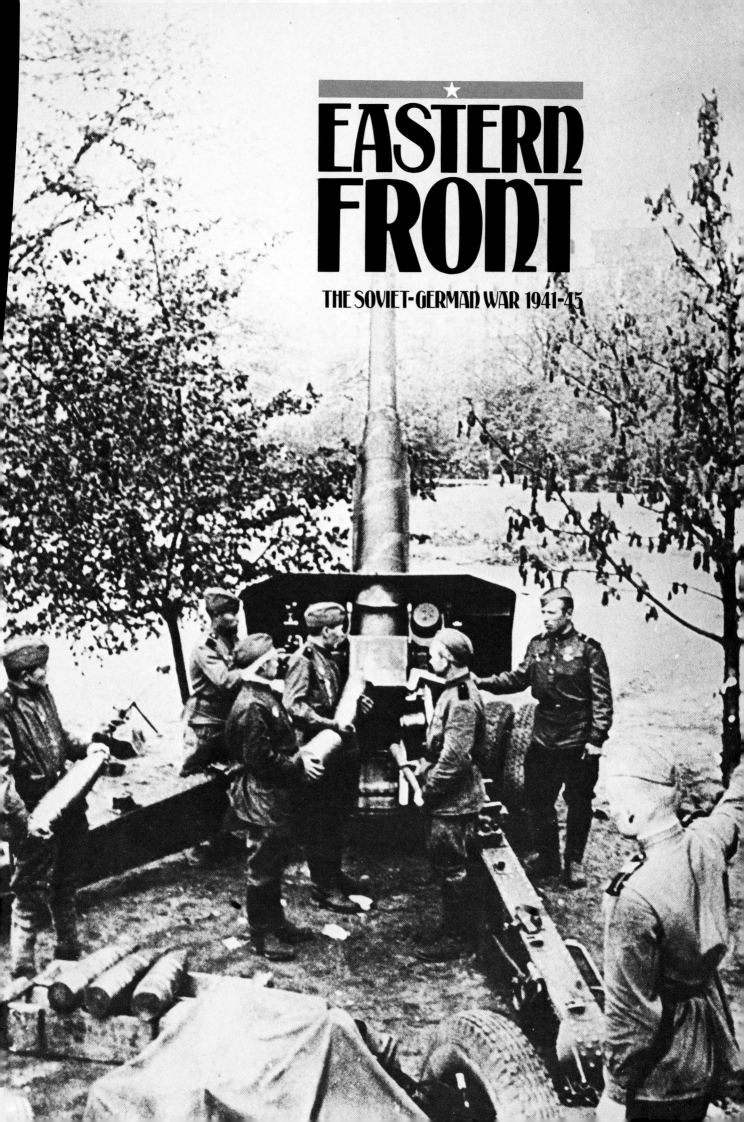

EASTERN FRONT

THE SOVIET-GERMAN WAR 1941-45

THE MILITARY PRESS

Distributed by Crown Publishers Inc.
NEW YORK
A Bison Book

EASTERN FRONT

FRONT

THE SOVIET-GERMAN WAR 1941-45

J N WESTWOOD

This edition is Published by
The Military Press, distributed by
Crown Publishers Inc.

Produced by
Bison Books Corp
17 Sherwood Place
Greenwich
CT 06830
USA

Printed in Hong Kong

ISBN 0-517-42314-6

Library of Congress Catalog Card Number 84-60740

CONTENTS

CHAPTER ONE
THE MISTRUSTFUL ALLIANCE

In war and diplomacy, dictatorships are said to enjoy great advantages over democracies. Decisions can be swift, and their execution rapid. Secrets are safer when the press is rigorously controlled. But dictators are no more rational than democrats and, with criticism in short supply, their mistakes are often big mistakes, and longlasting too. In 1941 the two most formidable dictators of the 20th century, Hitler and Stalin, demonstrated gross miscalculation in their mutual relationships. Hitler began a war he could not win; Stalin, after the rest of the world had learned that appeasement of Hitler did not pay, became the greatest appeaser of all.

But in the two years of diplomatic and strategic maneuvering which preceded the German invasion of Russia, at least it can be said that each dictator was wise enough to distrust the other totally. Both knew that Nazi Germany and Soviet Russia, despite or because of their common totalitarianism, must sooner or later come into conflict. But both got their timing wrong, Stalin passively and Hitler actively.

In the period after World War 1, when defeated Germany and Bolshevik Russia were the black sheep of the international community, they had been drawn together for mutual support. Military cooperation had been one of the benefits of this relationship, for Germany sought a way of evading the limitations placed on her armed forces by the Versailles Treaty, while Russia felt the need to modernize her forces and realized that the same Germans who had de-

feated the tsarist army would make ideal tutors. And so secret military cooperation commenced, so secret that to a large extent the German government did not know what its generals were doing. Russian officers attended German military colleges, German experts advised the Soviet armaments industries and provided designs for new weapons, including aircraft. In return, German troops were enabled to exercise in the expanses of Western Russia (where their officers became familiar with the terrain they would one day invade). Russia provided facilities for training with weapons banned by the Versailles Treaty, including submarines and poison gas.

This cooperation ceased when Hitler came to power in 1933. Stalin's misgivings were founded less on Hitler's ideology than on the obvious intention to rebuild German armed forces so that Germany would once again become a great military power. To Stalin, Hitler's success was both unwelcome and unanticipated; up to the last moment he had urged the German communist party to fight not the Nazis but the Social Democratic Party. The latter, obnoxious to Stalin because its very existence demonstrated that Moscow's way to Marxist socialism was not the only way, had wide popular support in Germany and had been the force best placed to halt Hitler's advance to power.

In his *Mein Kampf*, and elsewhere, Hitler had made no secret of his attitude towards Russia. Moscow, as the center of world communism, he

Previous page: **Heavily armed German infantrymen take a break. Russia is a land of long hot summers as well as long cold winters.**
Below: **Molotov (left) photographed with Stalin. One of Stalin's earliest associates, Molotov was appointed Foreign Affairs Commissar in time to negotiate the Russo-German pact.**

regarded as the source of that revolutionary Bolshevism which threatened the world and of which Germany had had some taste in its abortive revolutions after World War 1. It was as a declared opponent of Bolshevism that Hitler had won such massive support among ordinary Germans. His hatred for Bolshevism was deepened by the belief that the Bolshevists' leadership was dominated by Jews.

At the same time London and Paris sought an alliance with the USSR. However, such an alliance had little attraction for Stalin. For him, the problem was how to postpone a conflict with Germany, whose military power he feared. An alliance with France and Britain might well result, he thought, in a war in which the three countries would be fighting Germany but with the French and British role reduced to

Secondly, Hitler's hopes for what he described as Germany's future greatness depended, in his view, on the conquest and exploitation of eastern Europe; Poland, White Russia, Czechoslovakia, and the Ukraine were the nearest targets for this, but Russia-proper was also in mind. Lastly, the Slavic inhabitants of these lands were, in Hitler's view, inferior racial types whose only destiny could be as underlings of the Aryan Germans.

Hitler's first advances were towards the east. First Austria, and then Czechoslovakia. In the Munich crisis of 1938 Moscow was able to claim that if only Britain and France had shown a willingness to go to war for Czechoslovakia, then the USSR would also have joined in to block Hitler. However, Soviet actions at this time suggest that Stalin had no intention of risking war. Soviet historians have subsequently claimed that the British and French governments would have liked to see Hitler expanding eastwards; insofar as they naturally preferred an eastward to a westward expansion this is no doubt true. Nevertheless, an attack by Hitler on Russia would have been unwelcome because, in the assessments of that time, Hitler would have won and thereby strengthened his already threatening power.

The Munich agreement, which dismembered Czechoslovakia and in effect removed the powerful Czech army from the military balance, was followed in 1939 by Hitler's grasp of the rest of that country. Having lost their illusions, the British and French governments thereupon gave guarantees to Poland and Rumania. By announcing that they would intervene should either of these two countries be attacked, they risked a war for which they were ill prepared (and also provided evidence, which several post-war historians have ignored, that they did not welcome an eastward German expansion).

cheering on the sidelines. Moreover, although Stalin had a high, and misplaced, regard for French military strength, he had no confidence in Anglo-French strength of will; for this, likewise erroneous, assumption he had strong arguments, not the least being the Munich appeasement. To him, an understanding with Nazi Germany seemed a much safer bet, and he prepared a receptive atmosphere for the diplomatic approach from Berlin which seemed imminent. One indicative change was the replacement of his commissar (minister) for foreign affairs, Litvinov. Litvinov, married to an Englishwoman, had pursued an anti-German line at the League of Nations and, moreover, was Jewish. His successor, Molotov, was much more palatable to the Germans and moreover was second only to Stalin in the Communist Party hierarchy.

It was later said that one reason Moscow chose the German proposals rather than the British in the negotiations of early summer 1939 was that the British did not seem particularly enthusiastic. The German delegates came to Moscow by train and were followed by the foreign minister, Ribbentrop, who arrived by plane to finalize an agreement. The British did not send a foreign minister, only officials, who arrived via the White Sea by cargo liner. However, although this difference was noted, the choice of partner was determined by what Stalin considered was best.

The Anglo-French negotiators were unaware that a German delegation was also holding discussions in Moscow, so the signing of the Russo-German agreement of 23 August 1939 came as a surprise to France and Britain, as it did to the rest of the world too, including the Soviet people. The latter, having imbibed years of anti-Nazi propaganda, woke up to discover that Nazi Germany was now a

Above: August 1939; a study in smiles. Ribbentrop (extreme left) beams, his aide smiles, Stalin forces a mixture of amiability and wariness, while Molotov tries his hardest as the official photographs of the establishment of the Russo-German Pact are made.

Below right: Soviet troops examine the wreckage of a captured Japanese mobile HQ after the battle of Khalkin Gol in 1939.
Bottom right: The Germans recruited troops from many nationalities and racial groups, particularly later in the war. Here soldiers from Turkestan demonstrate their knowledge of the 50mm mortar to a group of senior officers.
Below: Map showing the stages of Stalin's westward expansion in 1939-40.
Opposite: 'To the West!' A Soviet poster of 1943, printed in 200,000 copies, proclaims that the USSR is on the offensive.

trusted friend. However, a population still in the throes of Stalin's great purge was unlikely to raise any voices against such a change of tack, and ordinary citizens had long been persuaded that 'Stalin knows best'.

The published agreement was a non-aggression pact, but there was a secret protocol providing for the division of eastern Europe between German and Soviet 'spheres of interest' (a euphemism, as it turned out, for occupation). The terms of this protocol were so cynical that even to this day its existence has not been revealed to the Soviet public. Poland was scheduled for division between Germany and the USSR, the Russian share being mainly those areas which before World War I were part of the tsarist empire as the Western Ukraine and Belorussia. Finland, Estonia and Latvia (all once part of the tsarist empire) were to be in the Soviet sphere, as was Rumanian Bessarabia. There was also a trade agreement, by which Germany would receive food and raw materials from the USSR, paying for them with exports of manufactured goods. The German contribution would also include military assistance: the new cruiser *Lützow* was given to the USSR, for completion with German help in a Leningrad shipyard, and submarine and aircraft designs were also handed over. The German navy was granted the

right to use the Russian port of Murmansk.

Japan, already a close associate of Nazi Germany, had been engaged in undeclared war against the USSR on the Soviet-Manchuria frontier. The Russo-German agreement surprised Tokyo, which is perhaps a reason why the USSR was able to negotiate with Japan a peaceful return to the status quo. This was signed two weeks after the Germans invaded Poland and was immediately followed by the Red Army's advance into the part of Poland reserved as a Russian sphere. Hitler had invited the Russians to invade from the east at the same time as the *Wehrmacht* moved in from the west, but the over-cautious Stalin, perhaps fearful of Japan, or that the French and British might send troops to Poland, had held back.

This was in September 1939. During the following year Stalin maneuvered so as to enhance Soviet security against attack from the west. In exchange for moving the German-Soviet frontier eastward from the Vistula to the Bug, the USSR was allowed to regard all but a strip of Lithuania as its sphere of interest. Pacts were forced on to the Baltic states of Lithuania, Latvia and Estonia which provided for Soviet bases in those countries. Bases were also demanded from Finland, with a withdrawal of the Russo-Finnish frontier away from Leningrad (which

Top: Red troops demolish captured antitank obstacles during the Winter War with Finland.
Above: A wrecked Finnish float plane. Note the Swastika emblem used by the Finns.

Hitler's quick victory over France in May 1940 alarmed Stalin, who had hoped for a long-drawn out struggle between Germany and the Western Allies. Suddenly, a German attack on Russia seemed a possibility. However, Britain's unexpected resistance was encouraging. World War 1 had seemed to prove that Germany would never win a war on two fronts and Stalin and his entourage believed that until Britain was defeated Hitler would never challenge the USSR. Stalin in fact felt that he was in a strong bargaining position; the German offensive in France had depended to a large degree on supplies sent from Russia and this dependence was expected to continue so long as Germany was at grips with Britain. The USSR not only supplied her own products, but also imports, thereby enabling Germany to overcome the British blockade; British rubber was one of the products obtained by Germany in this way.

From this imagined position of strength, Stalin risked irritating Hitler by taking more of eastern Europe than had been agreed in the Russo-German agreements. Using his newly installed bases as stepping stones, he occupied the Baltic states; these, after thousands of their leading citizens had been liquidated by the NKVD, joined the USSR as constituent republics. The part of Lithuania reserved for Germany was also taken, without consulting Berlin; Stalin took care to place his troops here before the German forces in France had returned home. At the same time, the USSR occupied not only Bessarabia, but also Rumania's North Bukovina,

was within shelling distance of Finnish territory) in exchange for a transfer of much of Soviet Karelia to Finland. Finland refused, and the 4-month Russo-Finnish war of 1939–40 resulted. This conflict revealed the weakness of the Red Army, but by dint of numbers a Soviet victory was achieved: the bases were established and considerable Finnish territory passed to the USSR, thereby strengthening the defense of the Gulf of Finland.

which had not been mentioned in the Russo-German agreement.

Neither dictator had any illusions about what was going on. Stalin, aware of Hitler's preoccupations in the west, was pushing as hard as he dared in the east to strengthen his position against a future attack which he foresaw would be led by Germany. Hitler privately referred to Stalin as a 'blackmailer', but his anger was probably not the reason he decided to invade Russia sooner rather than later. It seemed clear to him that the more Germany became involved in his war against Britain, the greater would be the leverage that Stalin could exert against him. He could be threatened by a stoppage of Soviet supplies, and should Germany be seriously weakened a Soviet invasion of eastern and central Europe seemed quite possible. In the two or three weeks following the fall of France Hitler began to consider an attack on Russia before, not after, Britain's defeat. His generals, enthused by their victory over France, did not discourage him. In August 1940 arrangements were made for moving strong German forces to Poland. On 18 December 1940, after a good deal of discussion, Hitler approved *Fall Barbarossa*, the plan to crush the USSR and to occupy it as far as the Volga.

In the meantime Hitler and Stalin continued to maneuver against each other within the bounds of the Russo-German Pact. To forestall the Russians and safeguard oil supplies, Hitler offered Rumania a pact, and his troops were allowed to enter that country. His Tripartite Pact of September 1940 with Italy and Japan again raised the specter of a two-front war for the USSR, with Japan invading from Manchuria and Germany from the west. Deliveries of the promised German manufactured goods to

Above: Red Army troops in a trench in the Karelian Isthmus. The well-designed Finnish defenses kept the early Russian attacks at bay.
Left: Despite being heavily outnumbered, the well-trained Finnish infantry were far more effective than their Soviet opponents.

Russia were allowed to lag far behind the promises of the trade agreement. Stalin responded to all this by occupying some key islands at the mouth of the Danube, and threatening to stop Soviet deliveries to Germany.

In November 1940 a truculent Molotov went to Berlin and had discussions with Hitler and Ribbentrop which were not amicable; one of these discussions took place in an air raid shelter during a British bomber raid. Molotov evidently took some satisfaction in reminding his hosts, who had been talking about the imminent dismemberment of the British Empire, that Britain had still to be defeated. Germany offered Russia membership to the Tripartite Pact,

Below: **Ribbentrop (center) celebrates the 1942 anniversary of the Tripartite Pact with the Italian and Japanese ambassadors.**

but the USSR imposed so many prerequisites, including a free hand in the Balkans, that her accession was clearly out of the question.

A few days after this unpromising discussion, the USSR offered her Slavic neighbor Bulgaria a pact. The offer was rejected, and in March 1941 Bulgaria joined Hitler's Tripartite Pact and allowed German troops to enter. Hungary, Rumania and the newly created puppet state of Slovakia had already joined the German side. However, when the Yugoslav government was induced under German pressure to sign the Tripartite Pact it was overthrown; the new

Right: **Molotov (left) converses with Hitler through an interpreter during his November 1940 visit to Berlin.**

anti-German Yugoslav government was immediately offered and accepted a Treaty of Friendship with Russia. But when Hitler invaded in April 1941 the USSR refused to help the Yugoslavs.

For centuries the Balkans were regarded by Russians as their own backyard, and Hitler's dominance of this region, and especially his rapid defeat of the Yugoslavs, the Greeks and their British allies, was alarming. Stalin at this point appears to have realized the weakness of his position. There was a sudden switch from truculence to subservience in Moscow's approach to Berlin.

There had already been signs of a softer Soviet line. In early 1941 a new trade agreement had been signed which seemed highly advantageous to Germany but much less so to the USSR. It incorporated compensation paid by the USSR to Germany for the 'unauthorized' seizure of that strip of Lithuania which had originally been destined for Germany. The Soviet authorities, partly by use of secret police coercion, ensured that deliveries to Germany of grain and oil received priority treatment in the Soviet economy. The British ambassador in Moscow, Stafford Cripps, was ostracized.

While Stalin was taking all possible measures to placate Hitler, more and more German divisions were arriving in Poland, East Prussia, and Rumania, and German photo-reconnaissance aircraft were penetrating deeper and deeper into Soviet air space.

Above: The crew of a bogged-down T-34 surrenders to the Germans. In the early stages of the war many of the Russian tank crews were very inexperienced and scarcely able to handle their vehicles.
Above left: Map reading during a training exercise. The quality of the German training methods gave their troops many advantages.
Left: An engine change for a Mark IV tank during operations on the Eastern Front. Note the 'short' 75mm gun.

CHAPTER TWO
THE BALANCE OF FORCES

On the eve of the German invasion the Soviet active army comprised an estimated nine million men, of whom about 4.7 million were stationed in European Russia; the recent hostilities with Japan had meant that sizable forces were in the Far East. The Soviet Union had over 20,000 armored fighting vehicles, and perhaps 13,500 military aircraft. Of the latter, about 10,000 were in European Russia, with 4000 based close to the western frontier. The German army at this time had about 3.8 million men, plus 150,000 in the SS formations and 1.2 million in the so-called Replacement Army (training units). The Luftwaffe had 1.68 million and the navy 400,000. For the Russian campaign the total commitment of men was to be about 3.3 million, with about 3300 tanks and about 2800 aircraft. Units contributed by Rumania and Finland, and later by Italy, Hungary, Spain and Slovakia, did little to reduce the imbalance between invader and defender.

Clearly, if numbers were the only determinant, Hitler could not win. But he believed he had two factors in his favor. He considered that qualitatively the German forces, in equipment, training, experience and leadership were far superior to the Soviet forces. And he counted on the advantage of surprise: the surprise which an attacker, able to choose the place and time of each advance, usually enjoys. With these two advantages he believed that Germany could defeat Russia before the latter's enormous reserves of manpower and material resources could be brought into play. Similar calculations had motivated the Japanese in their victorious war against tsarist Russia in 1904–05. Although, as always, there was a strong element of wishful thinking in Hitler's calculations, recent history had certainly emphasized the strengths of the German armed forces and the weaknesses of the Red Army.

The Red Army had its origins in the Civil War which followed the revolution of 1917. In this struggle it was ultimately victorious and the tactics it used became enshrined as war-winning formulae which only a socialist society had the ability to employ. Among the ingredients of this military philosophy were the stress laid on political education of the troops, the close control of commanders by

political commissars, and the primacy of morale over material; an army could fight barefoot, yet still win if imbued with the right ideas. Stalin had been a military commissar in those days, and had developed some strong ideas, though little military insight, which he retained in the 1930s. One of his early disputes with Trotsky had been his opposition to the latter's recruitment of former tsarist officers to lead, under political supervision, the Red Army. He had been attached to the South Western Front and the friends he made then, especially in the First Cavalry Army (commanded by Budenny, assisted by Voroshilov) became his military advisers after his assumption of supreme power. Budenny's cavalry army had seemed to play a crucial role at one stage of the Civil War, and it was later celebrated as one of the Soviet Union's legends. This had the effect of ensuring that the Red Army would have a strong cavalry component and, more important, reinforced the belief, fostered at all available opportunities, that under Bolshevik leadership there was nothing that the Red Army could not achieve.

Page 16-17: Mounted Red Army scouts of the Voronezh Front in 1943.
Opposite: A German position is strengthened with antitank mines.

Above: A newly built timber bridge spans a Russian river.
Second left: German tanks and infantry move in on a Russian village.
Left: Despite mechanization, horse transport was still vital for the German advance.

Above: Soviet heavy guns on parade in 1936.

Below: A captured German Mark IIIJ tank armed with a short 50mm gun.

In the late 1920s the Red Army was of about 600,000 men, with a strong cavalry element. Soldiers were conscripted from the cities, and from among the poorer peasants of the countryside. Richer peasants and surviving 'bourgeois elements' were conscripted into labor battalions. Officers were still largely men who had served in the tsarist army, often as NCOs, but there was a sprinkling of tsarist ex-officers among them. There were no officer ranks in the usual sense; all officers were 'commanders' who were not saluted and who ate with their men. Only in operations were they allowed to wear badges of rank. Meanwhile, as Stalin climbed to power, so did his old

crony Voroshilov. It was under Voroshilov's auspices as Commissar for War that Russo-German military cooperation reached its peak.

The termination of this cooperation in 1933 was regretted by both armies, but Russia retained the benefit of the former Russo-German joint tank training school at Kazan, the joint poison gas training center, and the joint air pilots' school. By this time, too, industrialization had begun to provide the USSR with an arms industry. Heavy metallurgical and engineering enterprises were being built.

Tension caused by the rise of Hitler and the pretensions of Japan led to an expansion of the Red

Army, which exceeded one and a quarter million men by 1935. But this enormous army was not as strong as its numbers suggested. Because of the scars left by Stalin's brutal collectivization of agriculture, the peasant conscripts, source of almost all the infantry, were largely alienated from the regime and from their officers (who came mostly from the towns). At the same time the exclusion of young men who had 'bourgeois' fathers meant that those strata of the recruit intake on which other armies relied for the more skilled arms, especially artillery, communications and engineering, were not used. The promotion to officer rank, often to specialist officer's rank, of unsuitable candidates was a result both of this shortage of talent and the political requirement that men of proletarian origin should be preferred.

With war seeming to become more imminent every year, the Communist Party, which in effect meant Stalin and his entourage, decided that revolutionary purity might well be sacrificed in the interests of military survival. From the mid-1930s a whole series of measures were taken to put things right. All classes of young men were made liable to

were mediocre. Most of the former tsarist officers had gone, although the majority of senior officers were Civil War veterans, of whom many could not see why the next war should not be fought in the same way as that conflict. Others were men who were younger and had risen rapidly because of their political reliability (which by this time meant unquestioning loyalty to Stalin). In the early and mid-thirties there had been a nucleus of far-sighted officers who were not afraid of new ideas. The world's first parachute troops had been Russian, strictly speaking, for in 1931 exercises Soviet infantrymen, harnessed to American parachutes, took off clinging to the wings of German transport aircraft, from which they dropped off, one by one. The use of massed tank formations and of motorized infantry, the advantages of close coordination between infantry, armor, artillery and air power, had been realized by some officers, and especially by Tukhachevsky. The latter rewrote the Red Army Field Regulations to accommodate the new ideas, but was then executed and his work undone.

The Red Army purge took place in 1937 and 1938,

Below: A Soviet T-28 medium tank, a type which performed satisfactorily against Japan and Finland but was outclassed in 1941.

conscription into the Red Army. Officers' ranks were established (and later that old symbol of tsarist militarism, officers' epaulettes, made their reappearance). Officers' authority was strengthened. They no longer ate with their men and soon a severe officer was regarded as a good officer; any friendliness between an officer and his men was condemned, and could have dire consequences. It was claimed that discipline must be extra harsh because the Red Army, unlike other armies, could not have the discipline enforced by class subjugation.

The higher direction of the Soviet forces was entrusted to the Commissar of Defense, who had eleven deputies, each representing a particular arm. In the late 1930s most officers, from top to bottom,

Left: German assault guns pause during their advance.

although it continued at a slower pace for some years afterwards. Tukhachevsky, apart from having a mind of his own, had fallen foul of Stalin and Voroshilov in the Civil War, and obviously outshone them in that campaign. He was accused in 1937 of spying for Germany and Japan and of planning to establish a right-wing Trotskyite counter-revolutionary whiteguard regime (whatever that might be) in Moscow. Other Red Army generals were arrested at the same time; interestingly, their nominal political supervisers, the high-ranking military commissars, suffered equally. By the end of 1938 about 35,000 Red Army officers had been purged (that is, shot or sent to camps of low survivability). Some were tortured so as to persuade them to fabricate false evidence against their comrades. The intensity of the purge was highest at the very top. Every one of the deputy commissars of the Defense Commissariat was taken, nine out of ten of the generals, and eight out of ten of the colonels. As a long-term student of revolutions, Stalin presumably realized that an army is often the one institution which can overpower an authoritarian government. His purge of the Red Army certainly made his personal power more secure, but it set back the progress of the Red Army at the worst possible time. Just as Hitler was preparing to demonstrate the cutting edge of his panzer armies, the Soviet military leadership fell into the hands of men who distrusted anything new.

A peculiarity of the Red Army was its establishment of political commissars. In the Civil War these had been trusted Bolshevik Party members who were attached to units with the function of political education (that is, persuading reluctant soldiers that they were fighting for the best of all possible good causes) and of supervising unit commanders (who,

Below: **German propaganda picture of an attacking infantryman.**

at worst, were thought likely to betray the cause or, at best, to ignore Party requirements in conducting their operations). Originally, no order of a unit commander was valid unless it was counter-signed by his commissar. In the early 1930s, when a greater proportion of officers were themselves Party members, this cumbersome requirement was relaxed, and in 1934 one-man leadership of units was virtually restored when the commissars were renamed 'political guides' and instructed merely to assist and advise the local commander. But when the Red Army purge was unleashed the commissars were restored to their former authority, so that dual leadership was once more the rule. Having two men in command of one unit is not a battle-winning formula, and the poor showing of the Red Army in the war against Finland was partly attributable to this state of affairs. The pre-1937 system of 'political guides' was thereupon restored in 1940. During the war there would be further changes, for in fact there was no arrangement which could both guarantee the Party's control over commanders while allowing the latter the freedom of action so necessary to carry out their operations successfully.

The prevailing military doctrine was that of the offensive. Although plans were formulated on the basis that war would start with an attack on the USSR by one or probably more capitalist powers, it was laid down in the Field Regulations that the Red Army would immediately take the offensive, carry the war into the aggressor's own territory, and there annihilate him. In retrospect, this doctrine can be seen to have solved, but only by evasion, a number of pressing problems, and it led to several decisions which proved near-fatal. Among other things, it meant that at all levels, from staff officers down to small units, the strategy and tactics of defensive operations received scant attention.

Stalin was very much in command of military affairs, especially after his purge had removed the top layers of the military hierarchy. Although a man of a certain shrewdness, and at times capable of grasping the essence of a problem quite rapidly, Stalin was ill-served by the men he chose to advise him. His chief Party assistant and adviser in military affairs was Zhdanov, a Politburo member with an insalubrious past and little competence. Then there was Voroshilov, likewise high in the Party and the Commissar for Defense. Voroshilov had won an inflated reputation as a cavalry commander in the Civil War and was a man of little imagination. In the early 1930s he opposed mechanized formations and finally succeeded in dissolving them; this was one reason why he was so hostile to Tukhachevsky. A truly evil man in whom Stalin placed great faith was Mekhlis, a former commissar of the Southern Front in the Civil War who took over the Red Army's Political Administration (that is, the organization controlling the political commissars) at the time of the purge. Sent to the Far East, Mekhlis had intervened in the successful battle against the Japanese at Lake Khasan, the main aim of his interventions being the launching of suicidal mass attacks on Japanese positions which would soon have fallen anyway. He then went on to organize the arrests of the Far East commander and his associates. More bad influence was exerted by Kulik, yet another of Stalin's Civil War cronies, who was appointed as the Deputy

Commissar responsible for artillery in 1937, filling a vacancy caused by the arrest of the previous incumbent. Kulik was a foolish man, and the confusion over the design and production of new guns were largely his fault. As a further negative contribution he felt honor-bound, as an artillery man, to hold back the development of tank forces; for him the tank was a dangerous, but inferior, rival of the gun, and he did not hesitate to tell Stalin so. Stalin eventually overruled him on this, but some damage had been done.

Whereas the Red Army gave a good account of itself in the border actions against the Japanese, it disgraced itself in the war against Finland. Possibly the Far Eastern pre-purge commanders, being far from Moscow, had been able to mold their divisions into a really effective army. Perhaps the fact that they were on the defensive, a stance acceptable despite the doctrine of the offensive because this was a very limited war, was significant. The final Soviet victory at Khalkin Gol was designed by a general of some considerable competence, Zhukov, who had survived the purge. Against Finland, in an offensive war, the Soviet commanders were initially unimpressive and, even if they had not been, the inadequate training of both junior officers and men, the poor equipment, and the fact that they were fighting an opponent far more determined than the Japanese, would have produced the same result. The first months of this war witnessed the virtual massacre of unwieldy, poorly commanded, Red Army formations which all too often were pushed into hopeless frontal assaults on Finnish strongpoints. The eventual victory over the Finns was achieved first by replacing Voroshilov as supervisor of the operations by Timoshenko, the local commander (yet another graduate of the First Cavalry Army, but with a certain ability), and then

Above: Members of an SS cavalry unit on a reconnaissance mission.
Left: A German 37mm antitank gun is brought into action during a street battle. Although the 37mm gun was obsolescent by 1941 it saw action in some numbers until the end of the war.

by the sending of huge reinforcements.

The poor showing of the Finnish War convinced Stalin, though not all his generals, that a radical change was needed. From early 1940 to the German invasion of mid-1941 conference succeeded conference in an endeavor to reach agreement on changes. At many of these conferences Stalin was a participant; his interventions were unopposed, for all knew that to arouse his irritation was to risk arrest and death. In spring 1940 Voroshilov was eased out of his post and replaced as Defense Commissar by Timoshenko, who was made one of the five marshals of the Soviet Union. This was a useful change, but its effect was limited because both Mekhlis and Kulik retained their influential positions. It was possibly Timoshenko who secured the release of some experienced officers who were still alive in the prison camps; about 4000 of these valuable men were freed and returned to their duties, although many more were never released. The creation of a properly trained officer corps was undertaken, with the military academies producing

Above: A Heinkel 60C floatplane serving with Luftflotte 5 in northern Russia in 1942.
Right: Inside a Soviet aircraft factory, showing assembly of Shturmoviks. Although first flown as a single-seat design the examples shown here are of the more important and improved two-seater type produced from 1942 on.

Below: The Soviet Il-16 fighter served very successfully during the Spanish Civil War but it was outdated by 1941, although still in service in large numbers.

modernized programs and receiving thousands of officers who, because of the purge, had been promoted to positions for which they had received no training. But like so many of the measures of this period, this came too late. Although everyone anticipated war, its coming as early as 1941 was unsuspected, even though the events of May 1940 intensified the Soviet anxiety.

Disquiet at the speedy defeat of France was at two levels. It had been confidently expected, on the basis of World War I experience, that the conflict between Germany and the Anglo-French alliance would be long and bloody; long enough to give the USSR time

to reorganize and re-equip her armed forces before the victor turned against her, bloody enough to weaken the winner as well as the loser. However, the fall of Britain, which in May seemed imminent, did not occur and as the weeks passed Britain's armed survival reassured the Soviet leadership which, again on World War I experience, was convinced that Germany would never again undertake a war on two fronts. For the Red Army, the most disturbing feature of the fall of France was its demonstration of the crucial role played by tanks and motorized infantry, for the USSR's nearest equivalent to these technologically advanced formations had been disbanded in the wake of the purge.

Some comfort could be derived, however, from the advances of the Soviet frontier which had been made in the preceding year. The Finnish war, shameful though it had been, had at least resulted in a wider belt of Soviet territory to the north of Leningrad. The acquisition of the Baltic states again provided a buffer zone against invaders; it was strongly believed that any German attack would be launched from East Prussia, and Soviet Estonia, Latvia and Lithuania now stood directly in the path of such an advance. Much of the Soviet defense effort of 1940–41 was devoted to the fortifying of these three territories. Such work included the building of bases for the Red Navy, which now had the chance to advance from the Gulf of Finland and base itself in the Baltic proper. Further south, the acquisition of territories previously forming eastern Poland appeared to create yet another wide buffer zone, although some Soviet generals did not look back on this expansion with undiluted pleasure. The move of the Red Army into Poland in 1939, although hardly contested by the Polish army, which had been already shattered by the Germans, had been accompanied by such confusion and misunderstandings that several Soviet units became 'lost' en route; if a more or less peaceful advance was mismanaged, movements in real war conditions seemed likely to be disastrous, so once again the urgent need to create an efficient body of staff officers became apparent.

More important, the advance of the Soviet frontier into Poland meant that the former defensive

line, consisting mainly of a series of fortified areas behind the old frontier, seemed to Stalin and his entourage to have become badly located. It was the new frontier, not the old, which they felt should be fortified. So long as the doctrine of the offensive was the Soviet military philosophy, and insofar as this doctrine was valid (which it never was), such a relocation of the defenses was logical. However, by no means all the generals favored this; or at least they did not wish to dismantle the old defensive line. Marshal Shaposhnikov, a former tsarist officer who had eventually joined the Communist Party, escaped the purge, and had become Chief of Staff, was a level-headed officer who, however, was not in the best of health in 1940. He had earlier failed to prevent the disbandment of the mechanized formations and now he was again unable to prevail against Stalin on the question of the frontier defenses. Stalin insisted not only that the fortified line be advanced to the new frontier but also, perhaps to make the decision final or to speed up the work, specified that the existing line should be dismantled as a preliminary. Thus for a period, while the guns and other equipment from the first line awaited emplacement in the new, there would be no effective line at all. It was characteristic of the way Stalin handled things that he entrusted the execution of this policy to the man who most opposed it, Shaposhnikov, who retired from his Chief of Staff appointment and was almost immediately entrusted with the frontier fortification work. As so many had feared, the German attack

Above: An Il-2 Shturmovik in flight. Armed with two cannon and two machine guns in the wings and a third machine gun in the rear cockpit in addition to bombs and rockets, the Shturmovik had a formidable ground attack capability.

Below: Ju 87 Stuka divebombers served throughout the war on the Eastern Front, particularly in the later versions designed for the 'tank-busting' role.

came before this work could be completed.

The reconstitution of an armored corps was confused and hurried, not least because the Soviet stock of tanks, while being as big as the combined tank strength of the rest of the world, was composed of too many different types, none of which was entirely satisfactory. In the early 1930s there had been three mechanized corps, but Voroshilov, who could soon point to the Spanish Civil War as a demonstration of the uselessness of such corps, had them disbanded, and their protagonists were arrested. It was held that the proper place of tanks was not in their own armored or mechanized divisions, but as tank battalions permanently attached to divisions or corps, and as tank brigades temporarily attached to infantry formations facing tasks for which tanks would be useful. Thus in the 1930s there had been three successive policies concerning the proper deployment of tanks and this could not fail to be reflected in the standard of training of tank officers and in the difficulties which attended the design and adoption of new tank designs.

The new re-established mechanized corps consisted of two tank and one motorized infantry

divisions. Nominally they had an establishment of 1031 tanks, but serviceable machines in such large numbers were not available in 1940. Soviet tank design was in fact one of the most successful departments of Soviet defense technology; there were gifted designers at work who had escaped the purges, and the nature of their task, which was the evolution of successive improvements rather than the creation and application of startling innovations, was well suited to the structure and circumstances of Soviet design offices in the Stalinist period. But because the Red Army and its political masters had no clear idea of how tanks should be employed, the designers and builders were considerably handicapped. As it happened, and as became startlingly clear later, at the very time when the Red Army was struggling, obviously chaotically, to re-establish its mechanized corps, the tank factories were receiving designs of new tanks which would prove to be the best in the world.

Until the mid-1930s tank design, like other weapon design, could rely heavily on western technology. In the capitalist world there were armaments companies whose home market had been severely reduced by depression and disarmament, seeking outlets abroad. Thus the USSR acquired the license to build the Vickers 6-ton tank, a potentially good design which had been rejected by the British War Office. About 6000 of these were built in the USSR as the T-26 and the design served as a model from which Soviet designers could learn, and then improve upon. American Christie tanks were also acquired, and their suspension/transmission design became standard for subsequent Soviet designs, leading initially to the BT designs. Light tanks of the BT series made up a predominant part of the tank stock in the late 1930s. In the Finnish War the medium T28 tank was used in quantity; this had three turrets and was designed for use against fortified positions. Its performance in that war, while not disastrous, probably was the cause of its disappearance from the production lines in 1940. Heavy tanks tended to be very cumbersome but the line of development represented by the 5-turretted T-35 was, fortunately, cut short after a good deal of expensive development, and simpler single-turret machines substituted. By the end of 1939 one of these was adopted for serial production, the diesel-engined KV-1 ('Voroshilov'), which was at least the equal of other powers' heavy tanks. With medium tanks, a new line of development was begun in 1939 with a series of four prototypes whose fourth model was the T-34. This was later to be celebrated as the most successful tank used by any army in World War II.

Opposite: Victims of the Katyn massacre disinterred by the Germans.
Center left: The remains of a Shturmovik after a crash landing. Shturmoviks were very heavily armored to resist ground fire.
Below: A T-34 burns after being abandoned by its crew.

Inset, left: Hitler in discussion with the OKW Chief of Staff, Keitel, at Hitler's HQ in July 1941.
Inset, below: Members of the political staff of the Soviet 18th Army in April 1943. Sitting, extreme right, Leonid Brezhnev.

Thus, in 1940, the USSR had an excellent heavy and a superb medium tank design. Yet getting these models, so urgently needed, into production, was a surprisingly slow process. Part of the trouble was indecision on the part of Stalin and his advisers, although to Stalin is owed the credit of continuing the development work on the T-34 at a time when the military were opposed to this design. The switch from producing one weapon to another, more advanced, design is always a difficult decision, because the changeover involves a disruption of factory routines and consequent loss of production. There is usually, as in the case of these tanks, an even more advanced design in the offing and therefore a temptation to delay the changeover for some more months, during which time obsolescent designs continue to be produced. However, with all this taken into account, the circumstances of 1940 were such that an immediate changeover to the T-34 and KV should have been made. As it was, only a handful of them were built in 1940, and they constituted only 9 percent of the tank stock at the time of the German invasion.

With guns, the interventions of Stalin seem to have had quite serious results. The Commissar of the Defense Industry was arrested when he disagreed with Stalin on choice of designs; Kulik was probably prompting Stalin in this. Two incidents demonstrate the muddleheadedness of the decisionmakers. First, just as it was decided to increase antiaircraft defenses, it was also decided to cease production of antiaircraft guns. This was not the only occasion when, to avoid the choice of whether to introduce a new design or to continue producing the existing model, the 'compromise' of producing nothing at all was adopted. Secondly, there was the case of the new design for the 76mm field gun. A design (E-22 and its modification USB) was adopted despite the opinion of artillery specialists that it was a defective design.

Antiaircraft defense was also hindered by the failure to develop radar as fast as possible. In basic research the USSR had enough talented scientists, but the environment in which they worked was uncomfortable. A civilian research institute at Leningrad was making good progress with radar development in the 1930s, but suddenly its work was halted and some of its personnel arrested; the background cause of this was probably the wish of the Red Army's signals and communications administrations to take over this work. After some time, during which no progress was made, the research was handed back to the civilians. But work was again held up when, for a time, an influential group of officers persuaded Stalin and his associates that radar was technically inferior to acoustic means of target location. In due course the radar specialists did produce workable models, but not in time to be of any use in the first years of the war.

The provision of motor vehicles had been influenced by Voroshilov's aversion to the concept of mechanized corps, in which motorized infantry was a main component. In 1940 motor transport was

Main picture, below: A Red Army unit makes a probing attack on the Bryansk Front in August 1943 during the Soviet advance after the Battle of Kursk.

made the responsibility of armored forces,' commanders, which meant additional worries for the already harassed tank commanders, while promising to deprive infantry formations of any motor transport. In any case motor vehicles were scarce and, usually, in bad condition. Like the existing tanks, motor trucks could run only a few hours before requiring maintenance. Truck drivers, like tank drivers, qualified after just an hour or two of instruction. However, the Red Army's heavy dependence on horse transport did have some advantages. The horse had the advantage of possessing no fuel tanks which might suddenly declare themselves to be empty. Secondly, in the spring thaw and autumn rains, horses were superior even to tracked vehicles and could provide a service when motor transport was entirely bogged down.

The Red Air Force, which was organizationally part of the Red Army and regarded as an adjunct to the land forces, was the world's largest in terms of aircraft numbers. But, like the tank forces, this numerical superiority was undermined by the obsolescence of most of its equipment. Again, as with tank production, it was difficult to make the changeover from obsolescent but familiar types to entirely new designs, which initially would be built at a slower rate and were unfamiliar to most of the men who would have to operate them. In general, it might be said that the changeover to new types was too long delayed and this seems to have been a result of procrastination as much as technical factors.

A special ministry, the Commissariat of the Aviation Industry, had been established in the late 1930s with the object of speeding up the growth, both numerical and technical, of the air force. In 1940 a further reorganization resulted in the creation of a Defense Industry Council, directly responsible to the Council of People's Commissars (Ministers). In this, aviation had a department to itself (the other departments were for weaponry, ammunition, and shipbuilding). At the same time another body, the Defense Committee, had wide powers to enlarge the aircraft industry. By 1941 many new factories for aircraft and aircraft components had been built, especially in eastern regions beyond the effective range of German bombers. Nevertheless, in 1941 the Luftwaffe found itself engaged against Soviet aircraft which were technically inferior, some pathetically so. Production lines were only just turning over to new types.

How far Stalin's purges had been responsible for this state of affairs is unclear. A regime which could arrest its Commissar of Armament Industry just a few days before the Germans invaded was clearly one in which political absurdities might prevail over military realities. One of the foremost aircraft designers, Tupolev, is known to have been under arrest in this period, together with several other lesser designers and perhaps hundreds of their staff. Many, including Tupolev, were organized by the NKVD into design bureaux supervised by secret police officials, and told to produce designs of a certain specification. That these incarcerated designers did eventually produce aircraft designs good enough to be put into production does not prove that their imprisonment helped to concentrate their minds. However, the whole procedure does demonstrate the urgency with which the leadership demanded better aircraft.

Tupolev had built much of his reputation on the construction of heavy bombers but, as with other powers (including Germany), the long-distance heavy bomber had lost its attraction as a concept. The fate of the Soviet heavy bomber force was probably sealed by its poor showing against Finnish cities in 1939–40. But although the great Soviet aircraft of World War II bore the names of other designers, Tupolev was probably an influential figure in their development. The most promising new designs included Ilyushin's single-engine Il-2, or *Shturmovik*, a ground-attack fighter; this incorporated some of the lessons learned by the Red Air Force during the Spanish Civil War, one of which was the desirability of providing some armor against small-arms fire from the ground. There were also Petlyakov's Pe-2, a twin-engined fighter-bomber, and Yakovlev's Yak-1, a single-seater fighter which, although inferior to the German Messerschmitt Bf 109, was nevertheless a formidable machine when properly handled. At the time of the German invasion there were probably about 1500 modern fighters, including the Yak-1, in service, but the *Shturmovik* and Pe-2 were only just appearing in front-line air regiments. Most fighters were either biplanes or the Il-6; after June 1941 a frequent complaint was that Soviet fighters were slower than the German bombers, which for the most part was true. However, the Il-6, which had proved itself in Spain, almost made up in maneuverability what it lacked in speed. In the main, aircraft performance

Below: A wrecked bridge presents an obstacle to the German advance in 1941.

was limited by the unavailability of engines with as good a power-weight ratio as German aero engines. However this gap was gradually narrowed, and the Soviet aircraft engine designs benefited from German models provided under the terms of the Russo-German Pact of 1939. Operationally, a considerable handicap (again paralleling the situation in the tank forces) was the backwardness of the Soviet radio industry. Whereas the pilots of the other powers kept in touch by means of radio, this was impossible for Soviet airmen because their machines were not radio-equipped. By the outbreak of war only squadron commanders had a radio, which was intended to maintain contact with the ground but more often than not was out of order. Pilots navigated by flying low and using ground maps, signaling to their neighbors by means of flares or other visual signals.

Well before the war Soviet industrial policy took account of a possible future war situation. Rapid industrialization under Stalin, even if undertaken for purely civilian needs, would have automatically increased the war potential. This was fully realized, and some comfort was drawn from the supposed ease with which many of the new factories could be converted to war production. In fact this process was not at all as easy as was anticipated; in particular, the conversion of tractor factories to supplement the existing tank factories would be beset by all kinds of teething troubles. All big factories had a military-economic plan, to be put into effect in a crisis and presumably describing the types and quantities of military products to be produced. In 1939 a small-

Above: A German infantryman emerges from a shelter in a camouflaged trench. *Left:* During the advance toward Kiev in the early stages of Barbarossa the Germans encountered heavy resistance in the town of Zhitomir and brought in artillery to help in the street-to-street fighting.

scale mobilization of industry appears to have been undertaken in connection with the moves against Poland and Finland. At the same time, many civilian factories were required to shift a fraction of their production to military requirements, in this way gaining experience and providing a small increase in the weapons reaching the armed forces. Factories were scheduled to produce items closest to the nature of their civilian work: typewriter factories

were scheduled for machine guns, sewing machine factories for gunsights, clockmaking factories for fuses, locomotive factories and tractor factories for tanks. Artillery was undertaken by farm and textile machinery factories, and by pump manufacturers.

The relocation of much of Soviet industry in the east has frequently been stressed as an important and very wise measure of the inter-war years. In fact this was achieved to only a limited extent. True, much of the heavy metallurgical industry was located in the Urals or beyond by 1941, but most war production was allocated to enterprises in European Russia. Only about a third of aircraft production was in factories safely located in the east by 1941. The question of establishing stockpiles of strategic raw materials had been raised in the 1930s; these were intended to guarantee supplies to war industry in the event of a war interrupting normal supplies. Stalin, it seems, rejected the proposal that these reserves should be located in the east; basing himself on the doctrine of the offensive, he ordered that they should remain in European Russia, and even specified that some items, like fuel and food for the Red Army, should be stored close to the western frontiers.

Whereas the Red Army and air force were in a state of disarray, not fully trained, still awaiting modern equipment, and feeling, despite the bluster of propagandists, a lack of confidence engendered by the purges and the Finnish war, the German forces were in fine fettle. When Hitler had defied the Treaty of Versailles in 1935 he could count on the availability of experienced ex-servicemen of World War I as a nucleus for his new Wehrmacht. Conscription, formally reintroduced in 1935, could quickly be stepped up to provide the numbers which were needed for the campaigns of 1939–40. In fact, the Blitzkrieg concept of warfare, using armor and aircraft to produce quick results in highly mobile, highly concentrated, offensives, seemed to make

Right: Limited arms production continues in besieged Leningrad in 1942, with schoolboys replacing the regular workers. *Below:* Mail call for a group of Red Army men during a lull in the fighting at the Battle of Kursk.

relatively small demands on manpower. When the invasion of Russia began most of the German forces had served already for at least a year, and were brimming with confidence reinforced by a self-admiration which the campaigns of 1940 had seemed to justify. Even the Luftwaffe, whose performance over Britain had plainly not been brilliant, had restored its reputation elsewhere; in the Greek campaign which preceded the Russian invasion it had taken on the Royal Navy in the Mediterranean, and won. The impressive feature of the German forces was not so much their equipment, which with some exceptions was run-of-the-mill, as the thorough training of the men. The German soldier was a man who could work together with any comrades he might come across, for all had the same training and the same standards, and yet at the same time he could build on this foundation to adapt himself to new or unexpected circumstances.

Although the overwhelming majority of German divisions consisted of footslogging infantry, most attention was devoted to the comparatively few mechanized divisions. These changed their composition during the war years, but in summer 1941 there were two basic types, the tank and the motorized infantry divisions. The former, the panzer divisions, contained a panzer regiment of about 160 tanks and a motorized infantry brigade. A motorized infantry division consisted of two infantry regiments, carried by motor trucks. Infantry armored personnel carriers were coming into service to replace the motor trucks, enabling infantry to move up alongside the tanks on the battlefield. For the invasion of June 1941 19 panzer and 14 motorized infantry divisions were allotted (as against 112 divisions of conventional infantry). Mechanized formations would have been more numerous if the invasion had been postponed for a year or two; inadequate production of tanks and trucks had held back their formation. There was also a reluctance to place too much burden on formations which might conceivably fall victim to a fuel shortage.

German tanks were very good, not only in their design and engineering and workmanship, but also in their technology. Even when in the closing years of the war Soviet tanks seemed to be superior, the German lead in special technologies, and especially in tank radio and optical equipment, was clear. For the Russian campaign the well-tried Mark III and Mark IV tanks, both 23-tonners, were mainly used. Compared to the Soviet tank forces, they were committed in small numbers and, being types which

were approaching obsolescence, they might have been vulnerable. But the Soviet 26-ton T-34 and the 46-ton KV tanks were only just coming into service, so they were adequate at least for 1941. The problems would arise in the following years.

In the German Army, although tanks were the leading antitank weapon, the artillery had a greater antitank role than in most other armies. The self-propelled gun, which was really a tank devoid of turret, was operated by the artillery as both an assault gun and as mobile antitank gun; in both roles it could operate alongside true tanks. The antitank service also had guns mounted on light tank bodies. In its self-propelled gun forces, the German artillery was well ahead of other armies; this was a weapon which could perform most of the roles demanded of tanks, yet was quicker and cheaper to build. Other armies, including the Red Army, soon imitated the Germans in this. On the other hand, orthodox German artillery was far from representing the best that could be achieved. Probably because of the emphasis on armor and aircraft, which were thought capable of carrying out most of artillery's traditional role, this arm had been rather neglected. Guns were still horse-drawn. Fire control methods were inferior to those of several other armies. Artillery, moreover, was a less independent arm than in other armies.

Below: Red Army sappers at work mining a forest road in Karelia in 1944.
Bottom left: A crack Red Army sniper mourns a fallen comrade. Both sides made very effective use of snipers, allocating them for a considerable period to particular sections of the front so that they could make the best advantage of the terrain and enemy dispositions.
Bottom right: Printers prepare an edition of a Red Army newspaper, part of the system of propaganda and political education.

Above: A battery of Soviet Katyusha rocket launchers. The Soviets employed a number of weapons of this type. These are the 132mm version with 40-pound warhead.
Opposite: Men of the Grossdeutschland Division plan an attack during the battle of Kursk.

Below: A rather primitive sound-location device helps defend Leningrad against German aircraft. The Soviets lagged behind in radar technology.

Most guns were attached to infantry formations and controled by the latter. Moreover, antiaircraft guns were allocated to the Luftwaffe rather than to the artillery.

The Luftwaffe had taken serious losses during the Battle of Britain, not least in trained aircrew. Nevertheless, it remained a self-confident and well-equipped fighting force. Moreover, the Battle of Britain had not been a fair test for an air force which had been built around the concept of a ground-support role for the army, as had the Luftwaffe. Its bombers had really been inadequate for the attack on Britain, but promised to do as well in Russia as they had in the several European military campaigns. However, at a time when aircraft technology was advancing, the Luftwaffe was still relying on designs which had been evolved in the late 1930s. But the Messerschmitt Bf 109 was still among the world's best fighters, and the Messerschmitt Me 110 was clearly superior to its Russian counterpart the Pe-2. The twin-engined bombers which had braved the RAF over Britain would not, it was supposed, have much to fear from the Red Air Force. Finally, there was the Stuka divebomber, which had proved so devastating against tanks and ships in the European

campaigns. This, the Junkers 87, was unlike conventional bombers in that its bombs frequently, rather than rarely, found their targets. It required highly disciplined, highly trained, aircrew, and Germany was not as yet short of those. In view of the obsolescence of most Russian aircraft, the German assumption that inside the area which could be covered by the Bf 109, German bombers would dominate the battlefield, was valid.

The industrial base behind the German war effort had extremes of strength and weakness. German talent ensured first class design and workmanship. German method and German discipline ensured that equipment would be used to its best advantage. German geography, however, ensured that raw material supply would always be a source of anxiety and vulnerability. Oil shortage was already a determinant of German policies. Despite expensive but effective manufacture of petroleum from German coal, and despite the success in keeping Rumanian oil supplies available to Germany, the feared shortage meant, for example, that a great German effort would be made to conquer the Caucasus, and that in the later stages of the war German aircraft would be kept on the ground when they were urgently needed to help the land forces. Iron ore supplies from Sweden were also vulnerable, or so it seemed to the Germans. Material shortages were one reason why the blitzkrieg-type short and sharp war was not only the preferred, but virtually the necessary, strategy; Germany's wars had to achieve victory before supplies ran out. Having adopted this philosophy, there appeared to be no need to maintain a large armaments industry and at the time of the German invasion of Russia the German economy was still largely devoted to peacetime kinds of production. This was good for morale at home, but by the end of 1941 was creating serious supply difficulties for the German armed forces.

In 1938 Hitler had appointed himself Commander in Chief of all German forces and created a staff organization (OKW) to serve him in this capacity. OKW was a sort of war ministry, with some operational functions added. Keitel was its chief. The German Army was headed by its OKH organization, of which Halder was Chief of Staff in 1941, with von Brauchitsch as Commander in Chief of the Army. Hitler took a keen interest in decisions of detail as well as the more fundamental questions. In choice of weapons, perhaps because he listened to good advisors, he seems to have played a more useful, or at least less damaging, role than did Stalin in the USSR. The German military leadership was a mixture of sound professionals who perhaps did not like Hitler but were prepared to serve him, and of enthusiastic Nazis with more or less deserved military rank. The German forces were less plagued than the Soviet by incompetents occupying important positions. An exception was Göring, whose position in the Nazi Party and his intimacy with Hitler, combined with a boastful and unperceptive character, meant that the Luftwaffe received rather more than its fair share of resources. This share was often misused, and coordination between the Luftwaffe and the Army and Navy was poor, due to the personal animosity aroused by Göring and his cronies, and by Göring's unawareness that a problem of coordination actually existed.

Previous page: **A German assault gun in the early stages of the advance.**
Below: **Brauchitsch gives a lift to wounded in his personal aircraft.**

'Directive 21', the plan for the invasion of the Soviet Union, was signed by Hitler in December 1940. He decided to call the project Operation *Barbarossa*, Barbarossa being the popular name for Frederick I, a medieval king who had led Germans to the crusades. The chosen name was evidently intended to convey the historical, crusading, significance of the forth-coming campaign; it was to be not just a conquest like in France, but the annihilation of an evil and dangerous creed. As things turned out, the choice of name was appropriate, because Barbarossa had been accidentally drowned, somewhere in Asia Minor, while on his way to an anticipated victory over the Moslems.

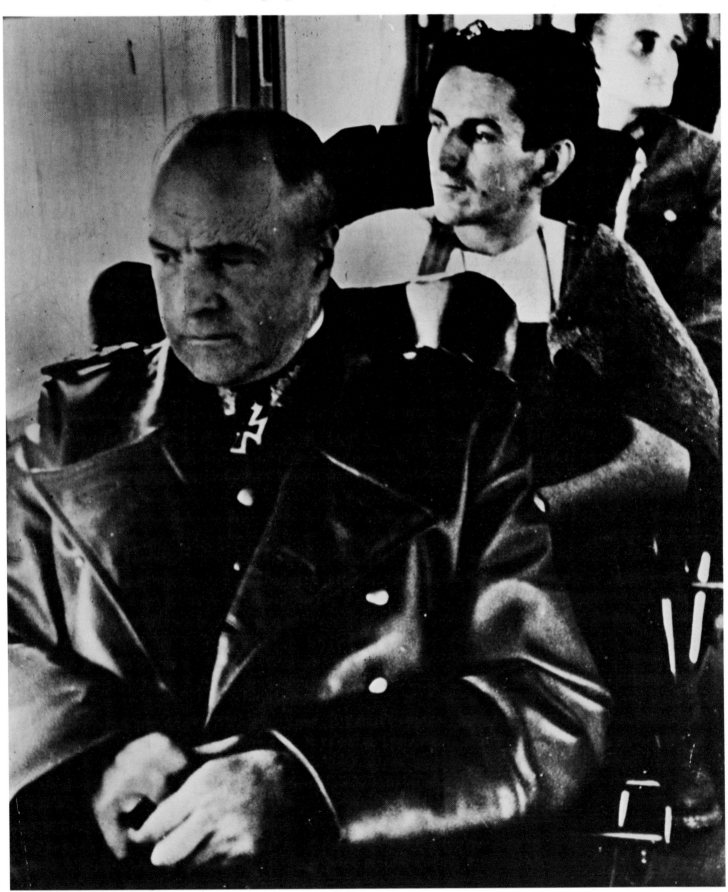

The decision to begin serious planning had been taken in July 1940, just a few weeks after the fall of France. Hitler's motives have been discussed at length since then, and several theories advanced. Because Hitler was very much a one-man band, with little record being kept of his discussions and thought-processes, there is ample scope for different opinions, but it seems clear that the decision to attack Russia was not made simply because in summer 1940 he had an army with nowhere to go. Eastward expansion and the destruction of Bolshevism had always been his obsessive goals, and the diversion of his forces against France and Britain he regarded as a temporary digression, designed to secure his rear before he dealt with the Soviet Union. Indeed, he had always hoped to avoid conflict with Britain. In the summer of 1940, while hope of a negotiated peace with Britain seemed increasingly unlikely, the inability of Britain to mount any large-scale attack on his rear while he conducted a rapid blitzkrieg campaign against Russia became clear. It seemed that the defeat of Britain was no longer a prerequisite for the invasion of Russia.

The basic structure of the *Barbarossa* Plan was the result of a good deal of controversy, and indeed Hitler made modifications to it not only when he finally signed it but also in the months that followed. Naturally enough, too, the date of the invasion was altered in the light of circumstances. But more interesting is the relationship between Hitler and his military planners in these months of debate. The generals, who had regarded Hitler's directives for the wars against Poland, France and Norway as dangerous gambles, seemed full of confidence about the attack on Russia. In their discussions there seems to have been no suggestion that this was going to be the most dangerous gamble of all. That Hitler had proved them wrong several times in the course of less than a year was presumably one reason for this; the surprisingly fast victory over France was also a cause for self-deceiving confidence. While they all knew that Russia was a far bigger opponent than France or Poland, somehow this knowledge did not greatly impress them in 1940; it was just one of several facts of technical significance.

Where the generals differed from Hitler was in the priorities given to different objectives. Not all the generals disagreed with Hitler all the time; indeed, Hitler's frequent changes of mind and the fact that not all military minds thought the same way, ensured that Hitler could always find one officer or another who would support his arguments. Von Brauchitsch, who as army Commander in Chief should have put his generals' arguments before Hitler, was usually only too anxious to avoid irritating the Führer. The result was that the army staff usually accepted Hitler's instructions but then sought ways to bend them towards their own point of view. This situation in fact doomed Operation *Barbarossa*, for both Hitler and the generals, each anxious to preserve freedom of action, had deliberately left undecided the final stages of the project; it was a plan without a conclusion, as the victorious German commanders discovered in September 1941.

The foundation of the plan, a three-pronged attack against Leningrad and the Baltic, Moscow and the center, Kiev and the Ukraine, was agreed by all parties, although this had not been the first intention of the planners. But the objectives of the invasion were not laid out in any order of priority. Essentially, the trouble was that Hitler wished to achieve too many things and, even when asked, refused to say which he regarded as the most important, on the grounds that all were achievable.

The long-term objective was muddled. There was

Below: The disposition of forces on 22 June 1941.

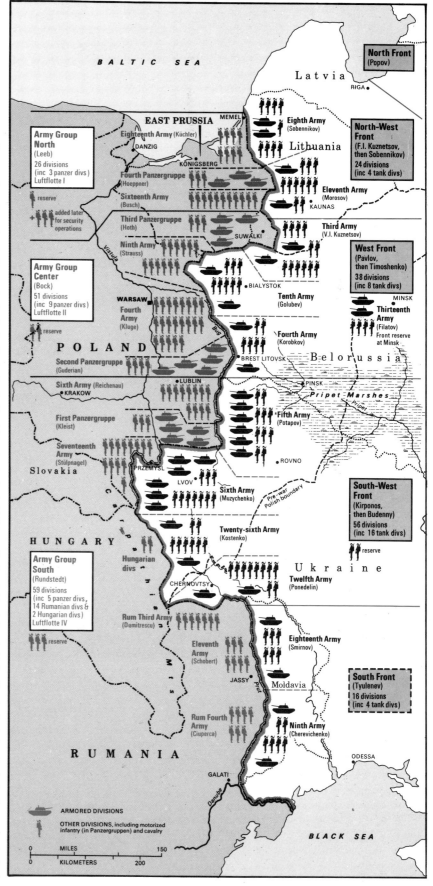

an intention to occupy Russia up to a north-south line which would mean (it was supposed) that any surviving Russian government would be confined to the east and deprived of the industrial base essential for carrying on a war. This line was to run from Archangel on the White Sea down to Astrakhan on the Caspian. One of Hitler's declared motives for occupying so broad a territory was his wish to keep Soviet bombers out of reach of German cities. It seems to have been a result of muddled, vaguely optimistic, thinking. Soviet industrial resources in the east seem to have been ignored, and no good reason was advanced for refraining from a total destruction of Russia as a state. What was proposed, although this was not admitted, was a partition of Russia which in the long-term could only have resulted in a threat to the expanded Reich.

This long-term haze was something the German generals could live with, as they devoted their professional energy to the immediate problem of militarily defeating Russia. For the generals, the utter destruction of the Red Army had the clearest priority. A super-blitzkrieg had to be waged so as to destroy Soviet military strength before the immense Russian reserves of manpower and production could be brought to bear. After all, Germany had 31 million males under 40 years of age whereas the corresponding USSR statistic was 74 million. Hitler, however, while agreeing with the importance of destroying the Red Army, also had other objects to which he seemed to give equal priority. Obsessed by his longstanding advocacy of expanding German *Lebensraum*, he seemed unable to grasp that the conquest of new territorial expanses was not a first priority, but would automatically result in due course from the destruction of the Red Army. Also,

preoccupied by German raw material shortages, actual or feared, he was over-anxious to send his armies to capture regions of great productive potential: the wheatfields of the Ukraine, the iron ore of the Don, and above all the oilfields of the Caucasus. Though these areas were economically (and hence militarily) important, their capture was unlikely to achieve what the generals rightly saw as the key to the whole campaign, the destruction of the Red Army. Hitler seemed possessed by other irrationalities. He was not greatly attracted by the prospect of capturing Moscow, but was obsessed with the apparent necessity to occupy or destroy Leningrad and Stalingrad. That these two cities bore the names of the two men whom he most abhorred seems to be the only explanation of this, although he gave other reasons; he said, for example, that Leningrad was so important in the history of Bolshevism that its fall would lead to a revolt by the Soviet people against the Communist Party.

The direction and course of the three thrusts prescribed by the *Barbarossa* Plan were determined largely by geography. Russia's western frontier in 1941 faced three states: Germany (that is, East Prussia, German Poland and German-created Slovakia), Hungary, and Rumania. Although Hungary was Germany's associate, the willingness of the Hungarian government to participate was by no means evident, so the attack had to be launched from German and Rumanian territory. The frontier totaled about 1350 miles, with the Russo-Hungarian frontier consisting of about 200 miles between the German and Rumanian sectors. By far the most important physical obstacle was the Pripet Marshes, on the Russian side of the frontier south-east of Brest Litovsk and occupying a frontage of about 150

Below: Unlike Stalin, Hitler visited his troops quite frequently. Here he meets some of his Eastern Front men early in the campaign.

miles. This area of streams and swamps, which in places was 300 miles deep from east to west, was regarded as quite unfit for tank operations and for large-scale infantry operations. The front was therefore divided into northern and southern sectors. The northern sector could again be subdivided. Immediately north of the Pripet Marshes lay the Orsha 'landbridge' (so-called because it was unbroken by the north-south rivers which provided obstacles elsewhere) through Orsha and its distant neighbors Minsk and Smolensk, over which passed the railway and highway from Moscow to Warsaw; it was therefore a classic invasion route, used by Napoleon among others. By this route Moscow was about 700 miles from the frontier. North of this was the Baltic area, separating East Prussia from Leningrad. The latter, Russia's second city, lay little more than 400 miles from the frontier. However, the intervening area was poorly provided with roads, and operations would be complicated by swamps and forests. South of the Pripet Marshes was the Ukraine. In the north Ukraine the terrain was undulating and partly under forest, but the greater part, down to the Black Sea, was treeless steppe which made ideal tank country despite the obstacles of four major north-south rivers.

An important geographical circumstance, whose significance seems to have been minimized until after the campaign got under way, was that the frontier lay across the narrow waist of eastern Europe, where the Black and Baltic seas are closest. This meant that as the German advance proceeded east-

wards, the frontage would widen and thereby require ever-increasing numbers of men to man it.

The northern German thrust was to be made by Army Group North under Field Marshal von Leeb. It was to advance from East Prussia through the former Baltic states to Leningrad. Compared to the other two army groups, it was quite small, consisting of two armies plus a panzer group; that is, 26 divisions, including three panzer and three motorized. Like the other army groups, it had its own air fleet, provided by the Luftwaffe but under its command. The largest of the Army Groups, Field Marshal von Bock's Army Group Center, was to take the classic route towards Smolensk but with a far from classic order of march. Mindful of the overriding need, physically, to destroy the Red Army before the winter, this Army Group was to undertake a pincer movement designed to entrap and then destroy the large Soviet forces defending this part of the front. It was to be helped in this endeavor by the existence of the Bialystok Salient, a large area of Soviet territory protruding westwards, and which was a standing invitation for a cutting-off maneuver. Von Bock's forces (50 divisions, including nine panzer and six motorized) were divided so that the northern part could attack the neck of the salient from the north through Vitebsk to Smolensk, while the southern prong of the pincer would advance from Brest Litovsk to Smolensk, skirting the northern edge of the Pripet Marshes. When this operation was completed (that is, when the infantry had caught up with the mechanized forces which were to achieve the

Above: **Field Marshal von Bock (left) in conference with panzer group commander, Colonel General Hoth.**

pincer), it was Hitler's intention to transfer the panzer groups to the Baltic or the south so as to speed up operations in those two areas. This was a main disagreement between Hitler and the generals, which had been papered over in the directives so that it was merely laid down that such a transfer might take place, if ordered by Hitler.

Army Group South under von Rundstedt was to be divided between a southern and northern wing, separated by the inactive Hungarian sector of the frontier. From Poland it was to despatch one army, with panzer group, towards Kiev, and another army towards Lvov and Vinnitsa, while from Rumania one army, with a small provision of panzer and motorized troops and supported by substantial Rumanian forces, was to cross the Pruth River and then move into the Ukraine through Bessarabia. Von Rundstedt, in terms of total divisions, had more strength than von Bock, for to his 41 German divisions (including five panzer and three motorized) were added the 14 Rumanian divisions under his command. Of the three Army Group commanders, he was perhaps the most incommoded by Hitler's last-minute changes of plan, for the Führer, ever anxious about oil supplies, in spring 1941 decided that to make an armored thrust from Rumania might provoke the Russians into a counterattack, which could put the Ploesti oilfields in danger. Although this seems a highly irrational line of thought, it resulted in the panzer forces in Rumania being transferred to the forces in south Poland, and the Rumanian offensive being downgraded to a slow advance, at least at the start.

Finally, in what was clearly a sideshow, eight German divisions were to be sent to help the Finnish army conduct an offensive designed (by the Finns) to regain the territory lost to Russia in 1940 and (by the Germans) as a thrust to link up with the German attack on Leningrad and to cut the Murmansk Railway, which seemed the most important of the USSR's potential links with the outside world.

The German commitment of troops, compared to the task facing them, was small. Of the total German army, one third could not be used as it was distributed throughout Europe to meet possible British attacks. Although the Luftwaffe allocated 2770 first-line aircraft to the campaign, another 1500 were left in the west to face Britain. Although about 3300 tanks were to be sent across the frontier, this was small in comparison with the Russian stock and even more in relation to the area of battle; after all, on the far smaller French battlefront in 1940, as many as 2800 tanks had been used. But it was confidently expected that the superior quality of German men and weapons would be decisive, as they had been in previous campaigns. The encircling of whole Russian armies was confidently anticipated; apart from the two-pronged pincer to be undertaken by Army Group Center, single-prong movements, with the sea forming the second prong, were envisaged in the north, where Hitler was confident the Russians would stand and fight in the Baltic states and thereby fall into encirclement, and the south, where the Black Sea would cut off the Red Army's retreat. The intention was to achieve victory in 1941. Since the spring thaw and the autumn rains were expected to make most of Russia impassable, this meant that this war had to be won within a few months. Indeed,

essential materials like fuel, not to speak of winter clothing, were not available for a longer campaign. What would happen after the victory was achieved, if Russia continued to fight, was unclear. Nor was there a very clear idea of what Russia was like; German intelligence had failed to produce either a clear or an accurate picture.

One additional factor on which the German planners relied was the achievement of tactical surprise. It was believed, rightly, that the Soviet command would be able to forecast neither the nature nor the timing of particular attacks. In fact, the Germans enjoyed not only tactical surprise. They had never believed that the amassing of their huge invading army behind the frontier would pass unnoticed, and therefore they had concluded that the war would not take Russia by surprise. Again, they were right, and they could hardly have been expected to anticipate that, in effect, the Red Army would simultaneously be aware of the impending attack yet act as though it were not. This absurd posture of the Red Army must be counted as one of the most intriguing of Stalin's works.

In the first half of 1941 information of Hitler's intention was received in Moscow from many sources. Not only were there many Soviet agents distributed throughout the world in key positions, but foreign governments were often willing to pass on to Moscow information which their own diplomats had picked up. In fact, the first level-headed appreciation of Hitler's preparations for attack seems to have been sent to Moscow by the US State Department, using contacts which the US embassy in Berlin had made with anti-Nazi German officials. Soviet espionage abroad was divided between the GRU (military intelligence) and the NKVD (state security). The former had lost some good analysts during the purges, but this was not the reason why knowledge of German designs was somehow not passed on to the Soviet armed forces. Indeed, the GRU operatives included Richard Sorge, working in Tokyo and

Opposite: Field Marshal von Rundstedt, facing the camera, at his headquarters in 1941. *Below:* Richard Sorge, the most successful of Soviet spies, who, before his arrest and execution, transmitted from Tokyo important information about German intentions. His reports on Japanese movements also helped the Soviet leadership decide to move troops from Siberia in time to stem the German advance at the end of 1941.

having access to the secret communications of the German ambassador there. The defect lay not in lack of information sent in by the espionage networks, but in the misuse of that information in Moscow. GRU and NKVD data, together with material sent in by external agencies of the NKVD and other sources, was funneled to the Central Information Department; or at least it was supposed to be, but what happened was that much of it went direct to Stalin's own private secretariat, where it was seen, or ignored, by him alone. Sources that sent in information which conflicted with Stalin's idea of how things would develop were not only ignored, but henceforth distrusted.

In the spring of 1941 there was virtually a flood of warnings. The US again found ways to pass on information, including the item that the Swedish government had been told by its diplomats in Germany, Finland and Rumania of the preparations being made. Churchill's warnings to Moscow had no effect. This was partly because Stalin, not unjustifiably, regarded any such information emanating from London as tainted; the British clearly had good reason to damage Russo-German relations. Also, for some reason, a highly detailed warning which included specific information about German troop movements was not delivered by the British ambassador until it was out of date. How far Churchill actually believed that Hitler was about to attack is uncertain. In May, at least, he was very doubtful, dismissing General Sikorski's (the Polish leader in exile) anticipations on the grounds that it was to Hitler's advantage to negotiate from strength rather than actually make war.

To protect his southern flank, Hitler had persuaded the Yugoslav government to join his Tripartite Pact, whereupon Yugoslav patriots deposed the government and established their own, anti-Nazi, regime. Hitler then diverted forces destined for the eastern frontier to deal with Yugoslav resistance, and a quick victory was achieved. The significance of this was not that the start of Operation *Barbarossa* was postponed for a month (it would probably have been postponed anyway, not least because dry weather came late to Russia that year). What was important was its apparent effect on Stalin. The earlier accession of Yugoslav to the Tripartite Pact,

and the enticement of Bulgaria to the Axis camp a few weeks earlier, had alarmed Moscow, which in various ways made its displeasure known in Berlin. However, no material Soviet help was sent to the Yugoslavs for their short resistance against the Wehrmacht. Stalin had expected that the Germans would be occupied with their Yugoslav campaign for at least three months, which would have meant that the remaining campaigning season in Russia would have been too short to permit a German invasion before May 1942. By mid-April Stalin must have felt very vulnerable, no longer convinced that he had a strong bargaining position with Hitler. Soviet policy suddenly changed; muted defiance of Hitler was replaced by total acquiescence. It was indicated to Berlin that Russian supplies could be increased if requested. Stalin took over the chairmanship of the Council of Ministers from Molotov. He completed the peacemaking with Japan, signing a neutrality pact with that country in April. At the railway station he said personal goodbyes to the Japanese delegation, and took the opportunity publicly to assure the German ambassador and military attaché, who were also present, of Soviet friendship. 'Whatever happens', he said to the latter, 'we shall remain friends with you'.

About 17,000 trains had been needed to move the German formations to their concentration areas on the eastern frontier. Although during 1940 the Polish railway network had been refurbished with the aim of easing troop and supply movements, passing the extra military trains had not been easy. The railway system of Rumania had been even more inadequate, so it is hardly surprising that the troop concentration took nearly six months. Most of the German forces in Rumania had in fact arrived on foot from the Yugoslav campaign. Towards the end of May the infantry was assembled, and in the course of a few nights moved up to its final positions behind the frontier. The mechanized forces were a little later, but were in position by the middle of June.

During these months the Luftwaffe had been busy reconnoitering the frontier and the areas behind the frontiers to a depth of about 200 miles. These flights, which by the spring were almost entirely devoted to aerial photography, were impossible to conceal from the Russians, but as time passed it was evident that the Soviet forces were not going to take any action against them. The paths of these reconnaissance flights were carefully tracked by the Red Army, and traced on maps. Presumably this was intended to indicate what the Germans were most interested in. But the antiaircraft troops were under strict orders not to open fire on these aircraft. This order was unpalatable to Red Army commanders in the frontier area, but they knew that they might face a death sentence if they defied it. The Baltic Fleet, which was under the Navy Commissariat, took a somewhat stronger line, and actually persuaded the Navy Commissar, Admiral Kuznetsov, to issue orders that German aircraft reconnoitering Soviet naval bases should be fired on by antiaircraft weapons. But Kuznetsov, whose action had probably been reported by one or other of the NKVD agents in the Navy Commissariat, was reprimanded by Stalin and his order canceled. Even so, he succeeded in issuing an order that Soviet fighters should force down German intruders; but as this order forbade

Opposite: Official photograph marking the signing of the Soviet-Japanese Neutrality Pact in April 1941, Moscow. Stalin is seen with Foreign Minister Matsuoka. *Below:* A German Henschel 126 army co-operation aircraft at work. These slow aircraft were useful for reconnaissance where no aerial opposition was to be expected. They could carry a single 50kg bomb.

Left:
Marshal Semyon Timoshenko replaced the incompetent General Pavlov in command of the West Front soon after the German attack began.

direct fire being opened it was ineffective. One Soviet fighter did send a dozen warning shots in the general direction of a German aircraft, and a few days later the German embassy passed on a complaint that a German meteorological plane had been attacked over Libau. One general decided that at least it would be a good idea to impose a blackout at airfields and naval bases in his Baltic command; but again, after a few days, Moscow heard of this and ordered that full illumination be restored.

What Stalin actually thought at this time is uncertain, but from what he said it seems clear that he did not expect a German invasion in 1941. He believed that any German troop concentrations were designed to put pressure on him, to make him play a more helpful role; hence the stress he placed on maintaining prompt deliveries of the raw materials he had promised Germany. Those who passed on intelligence items were careful to classify those which conflicted with his view as 'unreliable'. Abundant information was received not only of the German intentions but also of their detailed planning. The gist of Operation *Barbarossa* was indeed passed on to Stalin but was described as a fabrication by foreign interests who wished to sow distrust between Germany and the USSR. Despite Stalin's reputation for shrewdness, it seems very likely that an element of wishful thinking, encouraged by his ill-chosen advisors, played a great part in his expectations; since the USSR could hardly, in 1941, endure a full German invasion, it was necessary to believe that Hitler would not attack at that time.

Stalin's great fear was that a war would be started by provocateurs, perhaps anti-Soviet German officers who would arrange some incident in the hope that an exchange of gunfire would rapidly become a full-scale and unstoppable war. Ever mindful of World War I experience, Stalin and his advisors believed that in the tense European situation a mobilization by one side must inevitably provoke mobilization by the other, thereby beginning an inexorable process leading to war. This was why Stalin and his entourage took such stern action to prevent any Russian unit putting itself into a situation which might lead to it opening fire on Germans. The arrival of Rudolf Hess in Scotland was, for Stalin, extra evidence that the British were up to no good, and would do anything to bring about a Russo-German conflict. Meanwhile, the USSR continued with its preparations to fight a war in some year after 1941.

Shaposhnikov's preference for maintaining the fortifications of the old Soviet frontier, with only covering forces behind the new frontier, had clearly been rejected by Stalin in 1940. This was not the least of Stalin's mistakes, for such a deployment was the best possible defense against a surprise attack; but given Stalin's conviction that a surprise attack was out of the question, his opinion in this matter was at least consistent. So, in 1941, the Red Army was deployed along the new frontier, with its uncompleted fieldworks, and its vulnerable stockpiles of materials and munitions. The frontier itself was manned by the frontier guard units of the NKVD, the best and most numerous part of the NKVD's own army. These frontier troops, whose main task was to render the frontier impervious (from both directions) could also keep the neighboring Red

Army units under observation as well as provide their chief, Beria, with all kinds of intelligence via the NKVD's own communications network. In the spring of 1941, as soon as the weather was suitable, renewed efforts were made to build strongpoints and fortified zones. In addition to the construction troops, other arms were drafted to this work, which no doubt kept them fit but also interfered with the training which they so much needed. Even horses and tractors allocated for gun haulage were sent to help this work, leaving much of the artillery immobilized. The use of NKVD forced labor may have eased the manpower shortage, but such labor was not efficient and the NKVD administration was not liked by the Red Army officers who were supposed to cooperate with it. In addition, due to the distortions of the Soviet economy (and also because of the exports to Germany), many necessary building materials, and notably cement, were in short supply. The cement shortage held up, among other things, the building of new airfields, because the latest designs of Soviet aircraft demanded concrete runways. The fortifications of the old frontier, the so-called Stalin Line, still existed, but were not garrisoned and were denuded of their weapons. The troops, who had been moved forward towards the new frontier, were largely untrained. Some key items of ammunition were in short supply (so that, for example, units might possess guns but have no shells for them). Motor transport was so scarce that even a key mechanized corps had vehicles for only about a quarter of its infantrymen. In June General Kirponos, well aware of the German concentrations opposite his sector of the frontier, moved some of his units into stronger positions. He was observed by the NKVD and reported to Moscow, which made him cancel this move. A few days later he telephoned Moscow for permission to move at least his specialist arms, but permission was refused on the grounds that there would be no war in the near future.

By mid-June it seemed that the whole world except the Russians knew that Hitler was about to invade the USSR. Many responsible Russians also knew, but could not say what they thought. There were plenty of indications. German reconnaissance aircraft actually landed in Russia by misadventure (their crews were for the most part liberated by the advancing Germans later). An anti-Nazi German printer brought to the Soviet embassy in Berlin a new German-Russian phrase-book he had been ordered to print; it contained sentences like 'Are you a communist party member?' and 'Hands up or I'll shoot'. On the frontier, where relations between Russians and Germans had once been so punctilious that they would salute each other across the barbed wire, German soldiers were now seen to make derogatory finger gestures at Soviet officers. In various places on the frontier, after 15 June, the roar of German tank motors could be heard as German armor moved to its start lines. From time to time a German deserter offered himself up to the Red Army, and gave the local commanders a more or less accurate appreciation of how and when the German attack would come.

The Defense Commissariat and the military command depended on information sent in from the frontier. They were denied access to the intelligence reports seen by Stalin. Here and there, in June,

generals tried to strengthen their position without attracting the attention of the NKVD. On 19 June Timoshenko actually took it upon himself to order the camouflaging and dispersal of aircraft, tanks and artillery near the frontier. In the former Baltic states, where intensive efforts had been made to build fortifications, the local commander tried to amass stocks of anti-tank mines: the Russian army had always been good at mining operations, but in 1941 this talent had remained unexploited, with the frontier area being more or less undefended by mines. Admiral Kuznetsov, however, was ridiculed in the third week of June when he tried to place the fleet in an improved state of readiness. Nevertheless, by telephone, Kuznetsov later made sure that the Baltic, Northern, and Black Sea squadrons would be maintained at a higher state of readiness.

Below: Georgi Zhukov, most successful of the Soviet generals of the war, photographed in 1941 when he did much to stem the German attack.

On 14 June, by which time several sources had predicted the actual date of the German invasion but had been brushed aside, the Soviet government published a statement which may be regarded as marking the lower depths of appeasement. The main point of the statement was to express the view that the rumors that Germany was about to break the Russo-German Pact and attack Russia were quite baseless, and that the German troop movements towards the east were, 'it must be assumed', irrelevant to Russo-German relations. This statement, published in all the Soviet newspapers, may have been intended to reassure Hitler of the purity of Stalin's thoughts, in which case the failure of Berlin to issue a suitably appreciative rejoinder must have been an alarming disappointment. Internally, the effect of the statement was to make it very perilous for a Soviet officer to make any preparations for meeting a German attack, for such preparations would be regarded as a betrayal of official policy. This statement has been accurately described as 'the final tranquilizer' administered to the Red Army.

On 15 June the German commanders received their final orders to begin hostilities at 3.30am on Sunday 22 June. As the weekend approached, local Soviet commanders saw and heard ever more convincing evidence of what was impending. By Friday some generals were signaling this last-minute evidence to Moscow. Some of the frontier troops of the NKVD were in various stages of alert. All this was in spite of an order which had reached units a day or two earlier, renewing the ban on firing at German aircraft and forbidding any concentration of troops in the frontier area. Evidently some generals were

prepared to risk trial and execution in the hope of averting the catastrophe so obviously imminent. However, on 21 June, in the late afternoon, Stalin at last decided that something was in the air. He instructed key party officials (the party district secretaries) to stay at their posts. In the evening he received Timoshenko, Zhukov (recently appointed Chief of the General Staff) and Vatutin (Zhukov's deputy) and members of the Politburo. The latest revelation by a German deserter was discussed and this time the generals stood up to Stalin when he said that this was obviously an act of German officers

Main picture: **German infantry trudge across the seemingly endless Ukrainian steppe.**

wishing to provoke a war. Finally, some time after midnight, it was agreed to send an order to the frontier units. This stated that a surprise attack was possible on 22 or 23 June, that units were to attain combat readiness, aircraft were to be dispersed, but no action was to be taken without further authorization. The likelihood of provocation was emphasized. Those units which received the order in time therefore had no guidance as to how to act in the event of a German attack. In the border areas, telephone wires were already being cut by infiltrators, so orders issued by local commanders in conformity with this

instruction rarely reached their addressees. Only the Red Navy, thanks to early instructions sent out by Kuznetsov, was in a state of readiness when the Germans attacked.

On 22 June, in the small hours of the night, the regular Berlin-Moscow passenger train rumbled across the bridge over the River Bug at Brest Litovsk. A little while later, the Soviet authorities sent forward a freight train carrying supplies to Germany, and this crossed the river frontier just as the German troops received their final orders. At this time, war for some German units had already commenced; the

Inset below: **The radio section of an artillery unit during the advance in the Ukraine.**

so-called Brandenburg Regiment, a code name for a special-operations unit composed largely of determined men recruited from Ukrainians, Lithuanians, Latvians and Estonians, was already at work. Small detachments of this unit had infiltrated the frontier by various means. Dressed in Red Army uniforms, many had crossed the frontier concealed in freight trains in the previous days. Their task was to cut telephone lines, spread false information, incapacitate the electric power systems, and capture important bridges so as to prevent their demolition by the Russians. In these tasks they succeeded very well. Communications between the forward Red Army units and the rear were so effectively disrupted that army commanders were virtually out of touch with their units from about midnight onwards.

In the far south, the Luftwaffe arrived a little ahead of schedule. The Red Navy at Sevastopol was aware of the approach of unidentified aircraft a few minutes after 0300 and, despite the unwillingness of certain officers to actually give the order to open fire, the ship and shore antiaircraft guns did fire. The Germans dropped some magnetic mines, and flew off. The local commander, Vice Admiral Oktyabrsky, thereupon tried to telephone Stalin. The latter could not be found, but his colleague Malenkov was brought sleepily to the telephone. Malenkov was unwilling to believe the message, replaced the receiver, and made enquiries. By that time all along the frontier and beyond, the bulk of the German bombers were making their approaches, observing their schedules more exactly. Many of them had crossed the frontier earlier, singly and at great height so as not to cause alarm. They now swooped down on selected towns and, more importantly, on the 70-odd Soviet airfields which lay behind the

Below: KV-1 tanks lead a minor Soviet counterattack in the summer of 1941. Poor training usually doomed such attacks to failure despite the superior qualities of the few available T-34 and KV-1 tanks.

frontier and on which were lined up in neat rows the Red Air Force's first-line fighter aircraft. Within the course of half an hour the latter were out of action, and bombs were falling on the Baltic naval bases, and on cities like Minsk and Odessa.

Simultaneously the German artillery opened up on the Russian positions which had been plotted so meticulously over the previous few months. On the three fronts, tanks and infantry broke through the Russian positions. The NKVD frontier guards, for the most part, fought bravely but ineffectively, unable to prevent the Germans pushing through to engage the scattered and unprepared Red Army.

For some hours Stalin clung to his belief that since a massive surprise attack was out of the question, this must surely be a provocation. Red Army units still received no orders to open fire, although at this time many were in fact fighting fiercely because they hardly had any alternative. The army commander facing the German Army Group Center was specifically told that he was not to return German artillery fire. Only at about 0800 did the Soviet army commanders receive a directive to resist in full strength, but not to cross the frontier in pursuit. Stalin was trying to dissolve what he still called a crisis in Russo-German relations. His final attempt was to secure Japanese mediation, but this failed and so at noon the Soviet population was informed over the radio that Russia was at war. By that time about 1200 Soviet aircraft had been destroyed. So, until nine hours after the first bombing, Soviet radio stations had been broadcasting their normal programs. That was why the staff of the Soviet embassy in Berlin, informed that war had started but with their telephone lines cut, heard a rousing program of keep-fit music when they sought information by tuning in to Radio Moscow.

Soviet radio programs were customarily broadcast through loudspeakers in town squares and other places, and so the same keep-fit music, childrens' stories, and news of the latest Stakhanovites could be heard in frontier towns and barracks that morning, in the intervals between the explosions of bombs and shells, and against a background rumble of tanks and aircraft. In these places, littered with corpses and veiled by smoke, Red Army officers turned to each other and asked, 'Are we at war?'

Below: A corduroy road built by the Germans to help overcome the marshy terrain their advance encountered.
Bottom: A rare action photograph of a Stuka bomber at the foot of its attack dive over a Russian town.

Previous page:
**German infantry
advancing in open
order over the steppe.
Despite the much-
publicized successes
of the German
motorized forces, the
pace of the advance
was limited by the
slow-moving infantry
divisions.**
Below: **German
infantryman with MG
34 machine gun in
action outside a
Russian town.**

In 1941 the central German thrust, that of Army Group Center, was not regarded as the most important, but has since been portrayed as the key to the war. This is largely because the failure of Hitler's attack on the USSR, ending with the capture of Berlin by the Russians, has been attributed to the inability to capture Moscow in 1941. Many commentators, German in particular, feel that the fall of Moscow would have meant a Soviet collapse. This is probably a wrong conclusion, but it has been sufficient to launch dozens of postwar books, some by the generals involved, whose main object has been to shift the blame from one set of German shoulders to another.

In 1905 the Japanese, fighting the Russians in Manchuria, had fought themselves into a situation in which each victory they won and each advance they made only brought them closer to defeat. In 1941 the Germans rediscovered that Russia, because of its size and resources, was no ordinary enemy. But whereas it took the Japanese over a year to come face to face with this truth, some German officers were beginning to realize that they faced defeat after only

a month of fighting in which every week brought a fresh and unprecedented triumph. On the face of it the Russians suffered a huge military catastrophe in the first week of war. To take just one example, on the second day of the campaign, the German forces claimed the destruction of no fewer than 2500 Soviet aircraft; even the ebullient Göring refused to believe this, and ordered a re-count of aircraft wreckage which resulted in the figure actually being raised by a few hundred.

But the rapid advance and the huge destruction wreaked on the retreating Russians only concealed the fact that the objectives of the *Barbarossa* Plan, on which the defeat of Russia finally depended, were not being achieved. The first phase of the Plan had been given three weeks, after which the Red Army was to be shattered and the German line advanced to reach the rivers Dvina and Dniepr in north and south, and the city of Smolensk in the center. The next three weeks were to be spent in recuperation and consolidation, and the second phase, only partially planned, was then to begin. Thus the second phase, intended to finish the war, was to have

begun on 31 July but, as things turned out, on that date the first phase was still to be completed, and the German forces badly needed rest and recuperation. Phase 2 would have only a few weeks before the autumn rains set in, and the *Barbarossa* Plan was therefore in jeopardy.

The thrusts by Army Group North and Army Group South will be fully described in the next chapter. Briefly, thanks to the successful capture of key bridges, Army Group North's advance had been rapid in the first few weeks, and Red forces were in danger of being cut off in Estonia. Yet the aim of destroying the Red Army in this locality had not been achieved, despite the heavy losses of tanks and guns suffered by the Russians. Army Group South had undertaken two thrusts. That launched over the steppes had made slow but steady progress and seemed likely, eventually, to encircle Soviet forces on the Black Sea coast while the other, further north, had encountered Red forces which had seemed much better prepared to resist the invasion than others. Both these southern thrusts, therefore, had made territorial gains, and were promising to encircle hundreds of thousands of Red troops, but such decisive successes were still in the future, whereas the *Barbarossa* Plan had required their achievement in the first week or so.

Only Army Group Center, commanded by von Bock, had come anywhere near its targets. The *Barbarossa* Plan had proposed for this Army Group an ingenious enveloping movement designed to swallow the opposing Red armies and open the way to Smolensk and the Orsha landbridge, thereby putting Moscow under threat. This was to be achieved in Phase 1, with the pincers closed at Minsk, 250 miles east of the frontier. What would happen after Smolensk had been reached was not clear; Hitler had wanted then to divert this Army Group's armor to the north, to assist in the capture of Leningrad, and this intention was hazily included in the plan. But most of the generals favored an immediate advance on Moscow that would conserve the impetus of the German advance and result in the capture of the capital.

On 22 June the two panzer groups attached to Army Group Center began their respective advances on Minsk. In the north, Hoth's panzer group moved from East Prussia through Lithuania over country whose woodlands, and determined Soviet resistance, made progress quite slow. The vehicles were additionally held back because other German formations, and notably Luftwaffe trucks, ignored their route plans and invaded the few roads suitable for tanks, creating unanticipated congestion. However, Soviet counterattacks, though delivered bravely, were defeated because the Russian tank crews were clearly inferior in training and badly led. Soviet

Above: German forces move into a burning village past a wrecked Soviet armored car.

Below: A German flamethrower team prepares to make an attack in the summer of 1941. In the German Army flamethrowers were usually employed by assault engineer units.

Right: The first three months of the war. The map shows the three German thrusts and their success. Despite the succession of catastrophes the Russians maintain an unbroken line from the Black sea to Lake Ladoga. The Soviet term 'Front' corresponds to the German 'Army Group' but Soviet 'Armies' were much smaller than the German formations.

FINLAND

SWEDEN

HELSINKI

3 Dec 1941
Evacuated by Russia

HANKO
(USSR)

TURKU

VIIPURI

Gulf of Finland

LAKE
LADOGA

Lake
Oneg

Svir

Twenty-third
Army

Forty-second &
Fifty-second Armies

VOLKHOV

Eighth Army

LENINGRAD

TIKHVIN

Volkhov

Fifty-fourth Army

Fourth Army

TALLINN

NARVA

Estonia

LUGA

Luga

Fifty-ninth Army

Second Shock Army

NOVGOROD

TARTU

L Peipus

Eleventh Army

L Ilmen

BALTIC
SEA

VENTSPILS

PSKOV

OSTROV

STARAYA
RUSSA

North-West Front
(Voroshilov)

Thirty-
fourth Army

Lovat

Third Shock Army

KHOLM

OSTASHKOV

Volga

RIGA

Latvia

Dvina

REZEKNE

IDRITSA

VELIKIYE
LUKI

KALININ

Twenty-seventh Army

Twenty-second Army

Eighth
Army

SIAULIAI

DAUGAVPILS

Velikaya

BELYY

RZHEV

Twenty-ninth
Army

MEMEL

Army Group
North (Leeb)

Eighteenth
Army

Lithuania

POLOTSK

VELIZH

MOSCOW

Thirtieth Army

Nineteenth Army

Sixteenth Army

Fourth Pzgrp
Sixteenth Army

Neman

KAUNAS

VILNYUS

VITEBSK

YARTSEVO

VYAZMA

Thirty-second Army

EAST
PRUSSIA

Eleventh
Army

Twentieth Army

SMOLENSK

Ninth Army
Third Pzgrp

NOVI BORISOV

*Moscow
Highway*

ORSHA

YELNYA

KALUGA

GRODNO

Dniepr

Twenty-fourth Army

TULA

Army Group
Center (Bock)

Third
Army

MINSK

Berezina

MOGILEV

ROSLAVL

Twenty-
eighth
Army

Forty-third
Army

West Front
(Timoshenko)

WARSAW

BIALYSTOK

GORODISHCHE

NOVO
BYKHOV

Fiftieth Army

Tenth
Army

KRICHEV

BRYANSK

Fourth
Army

B e l o r u s s i a

Sozh

OREL

Fourth Army
Second Pzgrp

BREST-LITOVSK

PINSK

Pripet

Twenty-
first Army

BOBRUYSK

RECHITSA

GOMEL

STARODUB

Third Army

Second
Pzgrp

Thirteenth
Army

POLAND

Pripet Marshes

MOZYR

NOVGOROD
SEVERSKI

KURSK

KOVEL

Vistula

Bug

KOROSTEN

CHERNIGOV

Desna

KONOTOP

Sixth Army
First Pzgrp

Fifth Army

Fifth Army

BAKHMACH

Second
Army

Fortieth
Army

Seventeenth
Army

ROVNO

ZHITOMIR

KIEV

Thirty-
seventh
Army

LOKHVITSA

Twenty-first
Army

KHARKOV

LWOW

Sixth Army

BERDICHEV

First Pzgrp

POLTAVA

Psel

Thirty-
eighth
Army

Slovakia

TERNOPOL

KAZATIN

CHERKASSY

Donets

Twenty-sixth
Army

Dniestr

U k r a i n e

KREMENCHUG

Sixth
Army

Army Group
South (Rundstedt)

KAMENETS-PODOLSKY

VINNITSA

UMAN

PERVOMAYSK

DNEPROPETROVSK

Twelfth
Army

CHERNOVTSY

Twelfth Army

Yuzhni Bug

KRIVOY ROG

ZAPOROZHYE

HUNGARY

Rum Third
Army

Eighteenth
Army

Seventeenth
Army

Eighteenth
Army

Prut

Moldavia

Eleventh
Army

Dniepr

MELITOPOL

Eleventh
Army

Ninth
Army

KISHINEV

NIKOLAYEV

Ninth
Army

Carpathian Mts

Rum Fourth
Army

Ninth
Army

ODESSA

16 Oct

PEREKOP

Sea of
Azov

STALIN LINE

FRONT LINE, 21 JUNE 1941

" " 9 JULY

" " 1 SEPTEMBER

" " 30 SEPTEMBER

RUSSIAN COUNTERATTACKS

TRAPPED RUSSIAN POCKETS

RUMANIA

Fifty-first
Army

Crimea

BUCHAREST

SEVASTOPOL

0 MILES 200

0 KILOMETERS 300

Danube

CONSTANTA

B L A C K   S E A

commanders were additionally hampered by a flood of refugees, a breakdown of communications caused by sabotage and air attack, and by the freedom with which the Luftwaffe operated against them. To the south, on the other side of the Bialystok Salient, Guderian's armored forces, forming the other arm of the pincer, made somewhat faster progress. On his southern flank, bordering the Pripet Marshes, he deployed his cavalry division. This, the only such division in the German Army, was admirably suited for this swift advance through country unsuitable for tanks, although it would probably have succumbed to more determined air and infantry opposition; as it was, the occasional Soviet aircraft which attacked it usually managed to inflict quite serious casualties.

Meanwhile, following behind the panzers, part of von Bock's foot infantry consolidated the ring. The remainder of the infantry was engaged in creating an encirclement within an encirclement. Whereas the main encirclement meeting at Minsk extended 250 miles from the frontier, this secondary encirclement was of only about 100 miles, cutting off the western apex of the Bialystok Salient. General Pavlov, commanding the Soviet West Front, whose forces were destined to receive the main blow, had already deployed his three armies close to the frontier. In the confusion overtaking Soviet communications, and the chaos caused by the destructive German blows, it is not surprising that Pavlov heard about the secondary encirclement before he was aware of the panzer groups converging far in his rear at Minsk. Seeing his two most advanced armies threatened by the secondary envelopment, he ordered all his reserves forward to support them, thereby placing them even more securely in the German trap.

At this stage Guderian and Hoth were still thinking of making for Smolensk rather than Minsk, thus making the envelope larger. This had been discussed previously, with Hitler favoring Minsk and most of the generals favoring Smolensk. However, Hitler continued to insist that Minsk be the meeting

Below: Soviet partisans on the attack in Belorussia in 1941. Many members of partisan units were former Red Army soldiers who had become separated from their units by the German advance.

point of the pincers; he feared, probably rightly, that
an extension would so thin the retaining sides of the
envelope that the Red units would be able to break
out. The pincer was closed on 26 June. Guderian,
however, was allowed to send part of his force further
to the east in the hope of capturing river crossings
over the Berezina and, perhaps, the Dniepr.

On 28 June the German infantry had successfully
joined up to create the secondary encirclement. It is
not certain whether Pavlov knew of this; he did not
report it to Moscow, but this may have been because,
like so many other Soviet generals, he feared Stalin's
wrath. It was not until two days later that Stalin was
informed, and this information came not from
Pavlov, nor from the NKVD observers, but from
intercepted German radio transmissions. Zhukov,
the Chief of the General Staff, radioed Pavlov to ask
if the German claim was justified, and Pavlov told
him that it 'probably' was.

Pavlov was thereupon ordered to fly to Moscow
with his staff where he, and most of them, were
·forthwith executed. He appears to have been the
first, but not the last, to pay this price of defeat,
although his fate caused so much nervousness in the
army that subsequent executions were not publicized. From the top generals, subject to Stalin's
capriciousness, right down to the wavering foot
soldiers executed by detachments placed in their
rear for that very purpose, the Red Army was characterized by the large number of its men killed by
Russian bullets. Pavlov had fought his war for just
six days, he had been placed in a situation where he

could not possibly have won, and was an obvious
scapegoat.

Within a week the Germans had destroyed in these
encirclements two Soviet armies and parts of three
others, taking 287,000 prisoners. The Red Army lost
about 2500 tanks and 1500 guns. Few of the prisoners
would survive. As previously arranged, security
squads moved into the prisoner-of-war enclosures
and sought out political commissars and Jews for
immediate execution. The remainder were sent to
local camps or to Germany, where for the most part
they succumbed to hard labor and starvation rations.
The few who returned to the USSR in 1945 were
officially classified as traitors and dealt with accordingly. Many units within the encirclement escaped,
however. Some soldiers went to ground and re-
emerged later in partisan units. Others found their
way back to their own lines where they were inter-
viewed by NKVD investigators and, in many cases,
executed on fabricated charges of desertion or
cowardice. For the ordinary soldier, there sometimes
seemed little to choose between Nazism and Stalin-
ism.

While the German infantry was destroying the
Soviet formations within the encirclements, Hoth
and Guderian were pushing ahead towards Smolensk.
On the Soviet side Marshal Timoshenko, overseeing
this theater, was endeavoring to assemble new armies
to cover Moscow and hold the German advance.
Soviet counterattacks were desperate and usually
brave, but had little effect on the German advance.
On 16 July one of Guderian's motorized infantry

divisions captured Smolensk, that city already having been encircled from the north by Hoth's armor. Thus another encirclement had been completed, with the Soviet armies caught on the wrong side of Smolensk desperately trying to break out at the same time as new Soviet formations attacked from the east to relieve them. But as more German foot infantry arrived the prospects for the beleaguered Red troops became grim inside the Smolensk pocket. Their resistance ended on 5 August; they lost about 3000 tanks and 300,000 prisoners. Added to the losses previously inflicted, Army Group Center since 22 June had captured about 600,000 men and destroyed or captured about 5000 tanks. Moreover, Smolensk was only some 250 miles from Moscow.

Yet, taking the Russian campaign as a whole, the Red Army was far from defeated. The question of what to do next remained to be settled. The *Barbarossa* Plan, certainly, was worked out in fine detail, but its fundamentals appeared to be flexible. In particular, the question of priorities, on which Hitler differed from his more perceptive generals, had been fudged rather than resolved. The generals still felt that the prime objective had to be the destruction of the Red Army, and this had to be achieved so rapidly that the Russians would not have time to mobilize

their enormous manpower and production resources. Hitler at times agreed with this view, but insisted on giving other aims equal priority. That is, it seemed that there were at least three 'first' priorities. Hitler above all wanted to occupy those areas he regarded as of crucial economic importance: the wheatgrowing steppelands, the heavy industry of the Donets Basin and the oilfields of the Caucasus. Secondly, as stated, he attached obsessional importance to the capture of Leningrad and Stalingrad, regarding these two cities as the soul of Bolshevism. In any case, there was Hitler's crucial failure to realize that the first object would automatically assure the achievement of the other two. It meant, among other things, that he ridiculed his generals' preference for the main attack to be directed against Moscow. This, he claimed, would be merely a repetition of Napoleon's mistake. But the parallel between 1812 and 1941 was not valid, for Napoleon had not aimed at the destruction of Russia, and Hitler's generals had a good argument. Moscow, they claimed, was the one object the Russians would defend to the last; therefore an attack towards it would ensure that the Red forces would stand and fight, and it was only by inducing them to stand that the Wehrmacht could be sure of destroying them.

Main picture: Mark III tanks, one of which is burning, after repelling an attack by Soviet armor.

Left: A pontoon bridge supplements a timber structure at a river crossing. The Wehrmacht's heavy dependence on horse transport is evident.

The traditional
November parade in
Moscow was not
abandoned in 1941. As
a boost to morale it was
staged as usual, with
Stalin on the reviewing
stand.

The *Barbarossa* Plan had laid down, though not in a clear-cut sentence, that after the successful completion of the initial pincer movement the armored forces of Army Group Center would be diverted to Army Group North, which Hitler regarded as more important. That the generals, or at least those generals actually engaged in the center, had not accepted the downgrading of the advance towards Moscow, became evident in the first week of July. The first pincer having been achieved, Army Group Center wanted to allow its armored forces to continue by their own momentum. Hitler conceded this, and the result had been Hoth's and Guderian's achievement of another destructive encirclement at Smolensk. But on 23 July Hitler changed his mind. He now ordered that Guderian's armor should be directed south to capture Kharkov and to reach the Caucasus before the winter. The generals, although aware of the significance of Caucasian oil for both sides, found this change hard to swallow because, after a month of fighting, they were beginning to realize better than Hitler the enormity of the task, indeed of the threat, which the German forces faced in Russia.

Pre-war German intelligence had been hindered by the almost manic secrecy which surrounded all aspects of Soviet life, and the tight control which the Soviet government was able to exercise on movements of foreigners within its frontiers. Added to this was the tendency to filter incoming information so that items which seemed to clash with Hitler's preconceptions were quietly shelved. As a result, the German appraisal of the USSR's potential was wide of the mark, and this disturbing fact became evident to the Germans in the field, and then to army headquarters, OKH, in the first weeks of the campaign. A major miscalculation was that of the number of Soviet divisions. By the beginning of August Halder, the German Chief of Staff, noted that whereas about 200 Soviet divisions had been estimated, no fewer than 360 had already been identified in the course of the campaign. These divisions, it is true, were inferior in weapons, training and leadership, but they nevertheless existed and their destruction would require much time and resources. Nor, despite the many occasions when Red troops seemed only too happy to surrender, could it be said that the fighting qualities of the average Soviet unit were negligible. There were enough cases of heroic last-ditch, last-man, stands to demonstrate that so long as Soviet troops had some kind of resolute leadership, they would inflict significant casualties before they went under. Such resolute leaders were frequently the unit commissars who, knowing they faced execution if captured, could be relied on to keep their men in action, shooting the waverers to encourage the others. Despite the apparent ease of the great German victories, therefore, they were achieved at a cost

Opposite: A Henschel 126 reconnaissance aircraft on the northern front, its engine well-insulated from the damaging cold.
Below: A Soviet motorcycle reconnaissance unit operating near Mozhaisk about 100 miles west of Moscow.

A column of Russian prisoners, described by their captors as hastily armed civilians thrown into the defensive battle.

Colonel General Guderian inspects men of an SS armored unit.

which the relatively small German army could ill afford; by the end of July over 200,000 men had become casualties. Such a loss was not catastrophic, but replacements were less experienced and therefore, less effective and more likely themselves to become casualties. What was depressing for the German officers was that despite the huge totals of prisoners taken and armies shattered, the Red Army seemed to be able to call upon an inexhaustible supply of fresh men. The expected reinforcements from the Soviet Far Eastern armies were still in transit on the Trans Siberian Railway, but rail movements sighted close to the front suggested that the Red Army, despite its losses, still had an operational reserve; hitherto the possibility that the Russians could quickly raise fresh divisions had been rejected because of the anticipated lack of officers, NCOs, and specialist cadres.

The Luftwaffe was experiencing a similar situation. It had entered the Russian campaign with about 2800 aircraft, of which about two thirds could be regarded as serviceable at any given time. There were about 440 single-engine fighters (mainly the redoubtable Bf 109), less than 50 twin-engined Me 110 fighters, about 500 conventional bombers and 300 divebombers and over 100 long-distance reconnaissance machines available for service. These were opposed, it was estimated, by about 8000 Soviet aircraft. At the end of the first month the Luftwaffe had claimed the destruction of nearly 7600 Soviet aircraft, mainly by attacks on airfields. But the Red Air Force evidently still existed, and the estimate of its strength had to be revised upwards. Just as every military advance on land only revealed new and limitless fields to conquer, and every destruction of a Soviet army was followed by the discovery of another army ready to take its place, so the Luftwaffe discovered that no matter how many thousands of Soviet planes it destroyed, there seemed to be a limitless reserve of new Red machines and aircrew.

In the first month Soviet bombers, in slow, unwieldy formations, had been directed against the advancing formations in hopeless attempts to stop the Germans. Even had they reached their targets their bombs would have been poorly directed, for their equipment was inferior and their training primitive. In fact they advanced through the air like sacrificial lambs, being shot down *en masse* by the waiting German fighters. These bombers and their crews were lost for ever to the Red Air Force. On the other hand, because the majority of the Red losses were suffered on the ground, aircrews in general survived their aircraft and lived to fight another day. Since the Soviet aircraft industry was getting into the swing of mass production of new designs, this was an immense asset, as it meant that new aircraft could go into action virtually as soon as they were delivered. In the second half of 1941 production of each of the new designs rose from the hundreds to the thousands so that, for example, in these six months more than 2000 LaGG-3 fighters, 1000 Yak-1 fighters, and 1200 *Shturmovik* ground attack planes were turned out. Against this, the Luftwaffe was losing hundreds of aircraft (nearly 800 were destroyed in the first month) at the same time as new production was hardly able to make good the loss. The nature of the *Blitzkrieg* strategy, in which great victories were anticipated by the concentration of powerful forces over a short period of time, was both a cause and consequence of the virtual absence of a German war economy. Short victorious wars, it was felt, did not require massive armaments production while on the other hand the German economy, with its raw material limitations, was incapable of sustained mass production of armaments. The result of this was felt not only by the Luftwaffe, but by the tank and artillery arms as well.

By the end of July, therefore, the Luftwaffe had barely 1000 serviceable aircraft left on the Eastern Front. The demand of the army for ground attack sorties meant that attacks against Soviet airfields took second place, thereby giving the Red Air Force a breathing space. Although Soviet fighter pilots fought bravely despite the handicap of inferior

Left: A Soviet Tupolev SB-2 medium bomber and its crew. A fine aircraft when first produced in 1933, the type was obsolescent by 1941. A particularly poor feature was the inadequate 1200-pound bomb load.
Below: German infantry manhandle an 88mm antiaircraft gun over a pontoon bridge.

equipment, their toll of German aircraft was quite small. That German losses were nevertheless comparatively heavy is best explained by a high rate of accidental loss, and by the work of Soviet low-level antiaircraft fire during ground attack operations. Accident rates were bound to be high in operations over unfamiliar territory. Dive-bombing, in particular, was a risky business in which a pilot who was fatigued could easily destroy his plane and himself. In addition, faulty weapons took their toll. For this campaign the Luftwaffe was supplied with new types of antipersonnel bombs, which could be used by both bombers and fighters. These light shrapnel bombs were undoubtedly lethal to enemy soldiers within forty yards of their impact, but they were also dangerous to the German aircraft. All too frequently, with their fuses set, they remained attached to their carrier instead of dropping to earth. *Stuka* pilots could see when this happened, and take action, but other pilots were blissfully unaware of the peril; a

Below: A German Mark III tank copes with a typically poor Russian dirt road.

jolt was often sufficient to detonate these bombs, so aircraft touching down or flying through bumpy conditions were liable to explode for no apparent reason. With losses such as these it is hardly surprising that when Hitler ordered 'terror' raids on Moscow, the Luftwaffe was able to muster only puny sorties of thirty or forty aircraft to make raids which must have been more reassuring than terrifying to the Moscovites.

In fact, the Luftwaffe, as the Battle of Britain had demonstrated, possessed no effective heavy or long-distance bombing formations. Göring has since been blamed for discouraging the production of a long-distance four-engined bomber, the significantly-named *Urals* type. But Göring, perhaps because he was himself a flying man and a blusterer, saw through the protagonists of strategic bombing and realized that only a few bombers would actually hit their targets. The subsequent emphasis on dive bombing was therefore probably justified. Nevertheless, it is

unsurprising that the lack of bombers capable of reaching the Soviet arms factories was especially galling to the Luftwaffe officers.

It was galling, too, for the army. Soviet tanks, it was discovered, were not only far more numerous than the intelligence forecasts had indicated, but included new (T-34 and KV) tanks whose gun armament and armor protection were superior to those of the German tanks. In practice, better training and handling, together with the advantage of coordination by radio which the Germans possessed and the Russians did not, usually swung the result of tank battles against the Russians, even when the new tanks were used. Nevertheless, with about 1000 of the new tanks in operation at the start of the war, and with their production in Soviet factories planned to increase to over 20,000 units in 1942, it was evident that the Wehrmacht faced a very grave problem. Here again the lack of a long-distance bombing arm was, rightly or wrongly, bitterly regretted because the Soviet tank factories for the most part were out of reach of the Luftwaffe. What made the situation worse was that there was no immediate prospect of new antitank guns (to replace the inadequate 37mm model) or of new tank designs being produced in German factories. In part, the lack of a gun capable of penetrating Soviet tank armor was compensated when the rule against using antiaircraft guns against surface targets was relaxed; the antiaircraft 88mm gun did prove effective against the T-34 and KV. At the same time deliveries of even existing models of tanks was slow. Not only was production at the rate of only a few hundred per year, but Hitler wanted to use most of the new production in the Middle East against the British. On the Eastern Front, tank unit commanders like Guderian had to cope not only with sporadic fuel shortages, but a lack of spare parts which their machines, worn out by the dust as well as by their high mileages, badly needed. Hitler could not be persuaded that an increase of spare parts production, while reducing the output of new tanks, would actually result in more tanks being available at the front.

Below: A wrecked Russian train after a Luftwaffe attack. In general the Soviet rail system coped well with air attacks.

Russian sappers deal
with barbed wire
obstacles south of
Lake Ilmen in 1941.

Right: One of the
hundreds of Soviet
freight trains carrying
evacuated industrial
plant to the east in 1941
in order to restart
production in areas not
threatened by the
German invasion.

Not only tanks, but the essential motor supply vehicles, were in a poor state after a month of war. In Russian conditions tracked vehicles would have been more suitable, but these were lacking. Despite the use of French-built vehicles, and ex-British trucks captured in France, the Wehrmacht began the campaign with inadequate vehicles, especially in view of the decision to advance along the highways rather than the railroads. It was only the failure of the retreating Russians to destroy all their motor fuel dumps which enabled the supply services to escape a fuel crisis, but even so the belated discovery that the rough Russian roads meant that vehicle miles-per-gallon were halved came as a depressing shock. Those same roads also meant that there were requirements for repairs, spare parts and tires which exceeded all expectations. In the end some relief was obtained by using more rail transport. A few lines were re-gauged so that German trains could run right through, while a few other lines were operated with that part of the rolling stock which the retreating Russians had not destroyed or evacuated.

Thus the Wehrmacht's situation in summer 1941 was by no means as favorable as some superficial observers concluded. For this reason the front generals and OKH decided that, despite Hitler's declared intentions, Moscow should be captured immediately so as to bring the war more or less to a victorious conclusion. The campaign season was almost over. In the rainy and thaw seasons fighting would be impossible, and in the winter limited; yet in those inactive months the Russian factories would be busy producing tanks and guns and aircraft, while training units would be turning out fresh Red Army divisions at a rate which Germany could not match. A capture of Moscow would on the one hand draw in the Red Army's remaining reserves and thereby ensure their destruction, and at the same time strike a blow at Soviet transport, for Moscow was the hub of railway routes radiating in all directions. The moral effect of the fall of the capital would also be significant, and perhaps decisive. However, although the arguments began in late July, it was not until September that Hitler was persuaded to issue a directive aimed at the immediate capture of Moscow.

In the meantime three weeks of August were virtually wasted while Hitler and his generals argued about the next move. Admittedly, some of this time was put to good use for recuperation and re-supply, but since the 1941 campaign finally ended in failure

at Moscow when the weather changed, it is arguable, and has been endlessly argued, that those wasted weeks were crucial. In late August Guderian, despite an appeal in person to Hitler, was dispatched south with his armor to help in the forthcoming Battle of Kiev upon which Hitler had embarked. This battle, to be described in the next chapter, was probably the only large operation which could have been made at that time, given the precarious supply situation, and it resulted in an unprecedented victory. However, it did mean that when Hitler did decide to resume the attack on Moscow (meanwhile postponing the capture of Leningrad) Guderian's weary men and worn tanks had to rush back to the central front and could not go into action until the end of September.

The German plan was to use armor once again to envelop large enemy formations. On such a wide front two such pincer movements could be accommodated, one aimed at Bryansk and a second at Vyazma. On 30 September Guderian's armor pushed northeastward towards Bryansk, while von Weichs's Second Army moved southeastward to meet this thrust. Meanwhile the northern pincer (Hoth's armored group) and the southern pincer (Hoeppner's panzer group) made the Vyazma thrusts. Both of these envelopments were spectacularly successful, Vyazma being encircled on 7 October and Bryansk the following day. When the infantry had finished their mopping up, about 663,000 prisoners had been taken, with over 1200 tanks and some 5000 guns. These were astronomical figures, but they were not enough.

Orel had been captured earlier by Guderian, and in mid-October Mozhaisk (on the main highway about 65 miles from Moscow) was captured. Moscow was now plainly threatened and the Soviet government for the most part was transferred to Kuibyshev, on the Volga, and other cities; Stalin, the Politburo, and the military staff were not, however, part of this evacuation. But then the rains started. The German army, including its armored formations, was for several days bogged down at a standstill. When operations could be recommenced it was only thanks to the freeze which began in early November, and which within weeks brought its own serious problems. There was no winter clothing. German army boots (unlike the Russian) were well nailed and each nail conducted away the warmth of the foot. Engines of tanks, trucks and aircraft could be started only with great difficulty, and if not properly warmed could be put out of action completely. Some generals, including von Rundstedt, advised a halt, but were overruled. After all, Moscow was only 40 miles from the German advanced positions and just a final push seemed to be needed to capture it, and perhaps end the war. This final attack was called the 'autumn offensive'; this did not make the soldiers any warmer, but it might have cheered flagging spirits.

The plan was simple. Von Kluge's Fourth Army would press towards Moscow by the direct route with its 36 divisions of infantry, while panzer groups of Hoth and Hoeppner would encircle Moscow from the north, and Guderian's armor from the south. Despite bitter Russian resistance the two armored pincers made steady progress. Hoth captured Klin and by 28 November could see the towers of Moscow just 14 miles distant; Guderian passed Tula and approached Kolomna. However, the Fourth Army could hardly keep up with all this, thanks to Russian counterattacks. It finally struggled into the woodlands surrounding the Moscow outskirts, and in early December a few detachments entered the Moscow suburbs, from which they were soon driven out by armed workers. Then, just as German strength was fading, came intense frosts. Heavy snow had already fallen, blocking road and rail transport, and this final freeze, in which firearms refused to function and frostbite casualties numbered several thousands (including hundreds of deaths) came just as Marshal Zhukov launched a series of counteroffensives.

In the preceding weeks trains from Siberia had been running on to the Moscow Belt Railway, unloading their thousands of Siberian troops, before going back for more. These Siberians, together with local reserves, broke through the German positions at several points. Von Bock fell ill, von Brauchitsch departed, and Hitler took over supreme command (this made little difference, as he had been interfering throughout the campaign). Soon Guderian and Hoeppner were removed because they ordered withdrawals despite Hitler's firm order that there should be no retreats. Probably Hitler, whose frequent changes of mind had brought his armies to this edge of disaster, was right in this final judgment, for a general retreat could easily have degenerated into a rout. Instead, units were allowed to retire to forward supply depots, where they formed fortified areas, 'hedgehogs', each with its own stocks. Some of these, notably Kaluga, were in fact captured by the advancing Russians, but most held firm. However, in January the Red Army reoccupied Mozhaisk and was within 50 miles of Smolensk. Meanwhile, the USA had entered the war, and a growing number of Germans were privately coming to terms with the thought that the Third Reich had bitten off considerably more than it could chew. This included some men quite close to Hitler. Todt, the Minister for Armaments, gloomily predicted that victory would go to the most primitive contestant, the Russians, because their endurance, especially of cold, was greater.

Below: **Men of the Russian 20th Army attend a political meeting near Smolensk during the early stages of the final German drive to Moscow.**

CHAPTER FIVE

THE BALTIC AND THE UKRAINE, 1941

The Russian counteroffensive, whose strength and success were so unexpected to Army Group Center, was soon extended all along the front, from the Baltic in the north to the Black Sea in the south. In this way many of the gains made by Army Group South and Army Group North were lost, leaving the prospect of another gruelling campaign in 1942 and an end to the hope that 1941 would witness the crushing of the USSR and the concentration of the Wehrmacht on its other task, the defeat of Britain.

Army Group North, commanded by von Leeb, had done well in the first week of the campaign, but its subsequent progress was disappointing for Hitler, who from the first had regarded this thrust on to Leningrad as the most important of the three. It had been given three tasks, two of which were soon to be in conflict for priority. It was to destroy the Red forces in the Baltic region and capture Leningrad, on the way joining up with the Finns who would be advancing toward Leningrad from territory which, until 1940, had been Finnish. Prior to the invasion, the Army Group was assembled in East Prussia, behind the frontier and less than 500 miles from Leningrad.

Since 1940 the Russians had been feverishly strengthening their positions in the newly acquired Baltic states of Lithuania, Latvia and Estonia, which lay between East Prussia and Leningrad. The armed forces of these three states had been, almost literally, decapitated, with their officer corps killed or deported and replaced by Red Army officers. To these local divisions had been added true Red Army formations so that, in June, the Soviet North West Front possessed two armies, with Sobennikov's Eighth Army, near the coast, standing directly in the line of attack and the Eleventh Army well to the south. Although the terrain on which this campaign was to be fought resembled that of East Prussia, the German command seemed to ignore its unsuitability for tank warfare; the main attack was to be made by the Army Group's Fourth panzer group, with the infantry of Sixteenth and Eighteenth armies following close behind on a somewhat broader frontage. Rightly, it was believed that the key to a successful blitzkrieg was the rapid crossing of the two major river obstacles, that of the Neman, close to the frontier, and that of the West Dvina, about 200 miles distant.

Previous page: Red gunners try out a captured German 75mm antitank gun. This weapon was introduced hurriedly by the Germans in late 1941 when the previous types of gun were proving ineffective when faced by T-34s and KV-1s.
Below: Soviet mortars in action on the Northern Front, not far from Murmansk.

Left: Two British pilots of a Hurricane unit chat with Soviet air ace Boris Safonov at an airfield near Murmansk in 1941. Some 2900 Hurricanes were supplied to the Russians during the war and an RAF unit served briefly in northern Russia, partly in an instructional role.
Below: Alexander Pokryshin, a celebrated Soviet fighter pilot and leader, was eventually credited with 59 victories.

difficulty in defeating them with heavy losses. After this 2-day battle Reinhardt negotiated as best he could the marshy ground leading to the bank of the Dvina. To the south, von Manstein's panzer corps cut the main road between Daugavpils and Kaunas. Red Army units were withdrawing along this road and their artillery and tanks were able to inflict numerous delays on the German attackers, thereby enabling other retreating Red units to get across the Dvina. In order to capture the river bridge at Daugavpils, von Manstein sent two captured Red Army trucks, loaded with men of the 'Brandenburg' Regiment disguised as Red Army wounded. These trucks joined the flow of retreating Russians until they reached the precious bridge, whereupon they disembarked and captured the structure from its guard detachment. This success occurred on 26 July. It evoked great satisfaction on the part of Hitler; this

Above: Soviet naval infantry attack a Baltic island.
Top right: River crossing at dawn by German assault boats.
Right: Close-up shot of a heavily laden assault boat. The presence of the bicycles emphasizes the lack of mechanization of the German infantry.

On the first day of the invasion Russian resistance was faint and sporadic, but the broken country with its forests and poor roads made it ideal for harrying actions by small Red Army units which, for one reason or another, had become detached from their main formations. The Red Army was hampered in its movements by the stream of refugees; the latter comprised the thousands of Russians who had been drafted to the Baltic states to carry out the policy of russification; the original inhabitants, or at least those who had not been deported or executed by the Russians, stayed at home and, for the most part, welcomed the German invaders. Many of them, after all, were of German origin with German as their mother-tongue. Nevertheless the invaders were disconcerted to find that the local divisions fought better than had been expected. This was attributed to the presence of pistol-wielding Russian officers and commissars among them, driving them into battles for which they had no enthusiasm.

By the second day, the infantry marching along the coast had crossed Lithuania and entered Latvia, having marched about 40 miles in unpleasantly hot conditions. Meanwhile the two panzer corps had pressed ahead. Reinhardt's tanks fought a counter-attack by about 300 Soviet tanks and, thanks to the unimaginative frontal tactics of the latter, had no

Below: German 105mm le FH 18 howitzers in action.

was not to the advantage, however, of the generals in the field, for it encouraged the Führer to take a more personal role in directing this campaign, and henceforth the unfortunate von Leeb, who liked neither Hitler nor the Nazis, suffered almost daily interference as the Chief of Staff (Halder) listed the Führer's current anxieties. This, together with uncertainty as to what to do next, meant that as early as late June the German commanders were in danger of losing their momentum.

It was at this point that the question arose of whether the capture of Leningrad or the destruction of Red Army formations should have priority. Despite the early successes, only about 6000 Russian prisoners had been taken. The Red formations, though in disarray, still existed, were being reinforced, and were capable of weak but impeding counterattacks. It seemed, too, that the Soviet forces

Above: Food supplies
are shipped across
Lake Ladoga to
besieged Leningrad.
Right: Rumanian
troops cram an
inadequate road in the
Kerch Peninsula in late
1941.

in Estonia were going to stay there, where they could either be by-passed and thereby allowed to menace the German flank or they could be destroyed in an action which would undoubtedly be successful but which would delay the advance on Leningrad. Hoeppner, commander of the panzer army, and von Leeb, a traditional infantryman, could not agree either on objectives or methods, and their superiors at OKH were reluctant to make up their minds. Finally, Hitler made it clear that he would not risk an attack on Leningrad so long as the Red forces in Estonia remained battleworthy. At the end of July the Soviet position seemed highly perilous, with Army Group North pressing towards Leningrad and the Finns advancing from the north. But in reality the German campaign was already a failure, because the defending Red armies still existed and a link with the Finns had not been effected. These two objects were obviously attainable, but the *Barbarossa* Plan had required a quick decision. In the north, as in the center, the *blitzkrieg* had lost its *blitz*.

Hitler's assumption that the Russians would never evacuate their troops from the Baltic states proved false, and in due course priority was given to the capture of Leningrad. Already the two panzer corps had captured additional key objectives, seizing two crossings of the Velikaya River at Ostrov and Opochka in July. Only one significant river, the Luga, then lay across the German line of advance against Leningrad. But in early August, largely because of OKH and Hitler's vacillation, and partly thanks to the terrain and Russian fortifications, the advance temporarily petered out. However, the key city of Novgorod was captured, and by early September Schlusselburg, to the east of Leningrad, had been taken. This last conquest, in effect, cut off Leningrad. But Hitler changed his mind about what to do next. At one period he decided that Leningrad should be razed to the ground by bombing and shelling, at another that it should be subjected to a slow siege. This last decision enabled the armor to be diverted to Army Group Center for the attack on Moscow. As things turned out, the siege of Leningrad was to last 900 days, during which hundreds of thousands of its inhabitants died of starvation. But the German army never captured it.

By the end of 1941, then, a junction had been effected with the Finns, and Leningrad was isolated, but the anticipated crushing victories had not been achieved. Of the several reasons for this failure a lack of intelligence, in both meanings of the word, seems the most important. Lack of information about Soviet strength and dispositions was certainly a serious handicap, but failure to take note of what was known was even more serious. Above all, the nature of the terrain was no secret, and it should have been obvious that tanks would have great difficulties in the forests and marshlands. The state of the roads was also well-known, but the maps provided for German commanders gave little indication that the unsurfaced roads were little better than forest trails. Such tracks, and indeed the few surfaced roads, tended to be bordered by impenetrable forest, so any blockage could not be avoided by a diversion across the surrounding terrain. In the forests, abandoned Soviet vehicles were often sufficient to block for hours the advancing German tanks and trucks. A lone Soviet tank or gun could similarly hold up the German advance and inflict a little damage before being overpowered.

Far to the south, in the Ukraine, the lie of the land was quite different. Here the steppes provided fine terrain for mechanized warfare, but the immense distances imposed a different kind of drag, that of long and slow supply routes. Army Group South under von Rundstedt was more dispersed than the other two army groups. Partly this was because of the length of frontier occupied by Hungary. Hungary would in fact declare war on 27 June and would contribute troops, but at the outset was a neutral. Von Rundstedt's advance, then, was three-pronged. His Sixth Army under von Reichenau with a panzer group commanded by von Kleist advanced from Lublin, covering the Pripet Marshes with its infantry and threatening Kiev with its armor, before turning south along the Dniepr to cut off the Red Army formations north of the Black Sea. Meanwhile the

Below: German motor transport in the Ukraine. The Germans employed a large variety of vehicles, many of them captured in 1940 or produced later in French factories. This led to many problems with the availability of spare parts.
Bottom: Field Marshal von Leeb (center left) and Colonel General Hoeppner (center right) discuss the objectives of Army Group North in 1941.

Main picture: Russian Jews in German custody. From the very start of the German invasion the Jews were systematically persecuted.

Inset, below: Peasants welcome the German invaders. In many areas the Germans were at first welcomed by those with little reason to love Stalin but the Germans soon forfeited this support.

Above: A German panzer division on the advance, using both the main road and a nearby track. The vehicles are fairly close together, indicating that Soviet artillery or air attack is unlikely. *Right:* The battleship *Oktyabrskaya Revolyutsia* is divebombed at Kronstadt.

Below: An improvised bridge provides a crossing for a German light tank.

second prong, by von Stülpnagel's Seventeenth Army, was to proceed towards Vinnitsa, following a line south of that of the first prong. The mixed German and Rumanian armies were to cross the frontier a week after the other thrusts, and then move into the Ukraine, with the Rumanians additionally capturing Odessa, a city which the Rumanian government intended to have for itself.

All these thrusts made progress which was slower than expected. Largely this was because the Red Army's strength at the beginning of the war was much greater in this region than further north. Moreover Kirponos, commanding the Soviet South Western Front, seems to have been an exceptionally capable general; alone among his colleagues he was actually prepared and waiting for the German assault on 22 June. Against this, and the ever-oppressive distances, the Germans had the advantage that the Ukraine was perhaps the most disaffected of the nations comprising the Union of Soviet Socialist Republics. It was here that the advancing Germans were met with flowers and offers of help, and thanks for deliverance from the hated Russians. The Red Army was accordingly troubled not only by diversionists who wrecked its communications, but also by several uprisings of the local population. Such risings, however, were soon extinguished savagely by the NKVD. Kirponos also had the advantage that his area of activity was largely north of the steppe belt, in wooded and marshy territory unsuitable for tanks but quite well-suited to the Soviet style of warfare.

In mid-July Budenny, with Khrushchev as his commissar, arrived to supervise both Kirponos's South West Front and the South Front (covering the Black Sea). Henceforth, things did not go quite so well for the Soviet defenders. Hitherto the retreat had been fairly slow and with no catastrophic losses. The first major defeat came in early August, when more than 100,000 prisoners were captured by the Germans in the Uman pocket. By the end of August the Red Army had been driven back behind the Dniepr. A long withdrawal along the Black Sea was also necessary, although a strong garrison was left to defend Odessa. However, the Red Army, apart from the Uman disaster, had been spared catastrophic losses and in the course of its withdrawal had inflicted a steady toll of casualties on the Germans. It was at this point that Hitler decided to divert Guderian's armor from the Moscow area southward to Kiev so as to achieve another massive encirclement operation.

After battles en route at Roslavl, Krichev, and Gomel, in which the Red tank forces were defeated, Guderian forced a crossing of the Desna. Meanwhile, von Kleist's armor was attacking northward from Kremenchug and by 10 September it seemed likely that these two armored thrusts would meet about 150 miles east of Kiev. That city, the third largest in the USSR and the traditional center of the Ukraine, was regarded by Stalin as too important to lose without a fight. Budenny's requests for permission to withdraw were therefore refused; it was not until after Guderian and von Kleist had completed their pincer that Stalin reluctantly allowed a withdrawal. By then it was too late, and in the ensuing ten days not only was Kiev captured by the German infantry, but an unprecedented number of prisoners were taken (665,000 according to some accounts). Kirponos disappeared. Budenny had already been replaced by Timoshenko on the eve of this catastrophe. Guderian took his weary troops and worn-out tanks back towards Moscow.

In the far south the Red Army's withdrawal left the Crimea, as well as Odessa, as strongly defended points which threatened the German flanks. Hitler was additionally worried because he imagined that Soviet bombers could strike his precious Ploesti oilfields from Crimean bases. Moreover, he argued, conquest of the Crimea would open a short-cut to the Caucasian oilfields, across the narrow Kerch Strait. However, conquering the Crimea was not a simple proposition, for access to it was over the narrow (5-mile) Perekop Isthmus. The young Red Army had undertaken a similar operation against the Whites in the Civil War, and this successful storming of the Isthmus was in the inter-war years studied by successive generations of Soviet staff officers. Its defense in 1941 was therefore well-informed. The Isthmus provided very little natural cover, the defenders had command of the sea and, as often as not, local command of the air. Added to this was the traditional Russian genius for mining and it is hardly surprising that after a few costly and unsuccessful assaults some German officers would have preferred to abandon the enterprise, especially after the autumn rains had made prospects even worse. However, von Manstein had only just been appointed to take command of the assaulting army, the Eleventh, and he did not intend to begin his tenure with a failure. So, after a very costly yard-by-yard battle which lasted ten days, the Germans were able to swarm over the Isthmus and drive the Red Army defenders into Sevastopol. But before an assault on that naval base could be properly organized, the Red

Army, thanks to Russian command of the sea, was able to land a strong force elsewhere in the Crimea, near Feodosiya, so that Manstein, though in a strong position, had to divide his forces to fight, within the Crimea, a two-front war.

Allowing von Manstein's army to engage in the Crimean operation, which was not strictly necessary, was probably a mistake, for at this time von Rundstedt's main forces were making painfully slow progress and were in need of all possible accretions of

Above: A Soviet T-60 light tank in a recaptured village.

Below: A Soviet armored train in German hands after it had been disabled by air attack.

Above: Ribbentrop speaks in celebration of the alliance with Bulgaria at a gathering of Axis diplomats in Vienna. Seated, at left, is the Bulgarian Prime Minister and, at right, the Italian Foreign Minister Count Ciano. *Opposite:* A Soviet ski patrol in the forests of northern Russia.

strength. Some of his formations had been diverted to the Moscow campaign, and his Rumanian, Italian and Hungarian units were not always enthusiastic fighters. Hitler's intermittent interference, and a succession of rainy days in October, did nothing to speed the German advance. One result of this was that when the industrial Donets Basin was finally occupied it was discovered that in part of it the Russians had had time to remove all plant that was removable, and to destroy the rest. All the same, the invaders reached Taganrog and Kharkov by the end of October.

The next major city was Rostov on Don, capture of which would open the way to the Caucasus. In November, in bitterly cold weather, the assault on Rostov began. Russian resistance was intense, if not fanatical, with tanks sent down the streets literally to crush the German antitank guns, and each building strongly defended by determined infantry. However, after four days the city was captured, with about 10,000 Red Army men allowing themselves to be taken prisoner. This surrender may have encouraged Stalin to issue his subsequent savage directive in which, among other things, it was emphasized that a Red soldier who allowed himself to be taken prisoner would be regarded as a traitor (this not only made a POW liable to death or imprisonment if he were ever returned to the USSR but, under Soviet practice, rendered his next of kin liable to punishment).

Possibly it was in this spirit that the Soviet attempts to recapture Rostov were made. Certainly it is these attacks by masses of infantry, often primed with vodka, which are quoted as an extreme example of the Soviet practice throughout the war of launching successive mass attacks on impregnable objectives. All that such attacks achieved was the deposit of

heaps of dead Russians all around the German positions. Nevertheless, for other reasons, the Germans did abandon Rostov. What happened was that von Kleist's panzer army, which had captured the city, was well ahead of the slow progress made by von Reichenau's infantry. Timoshenko, further north, had succeeded in scraping together enough reserves for a counteroffensive. Although this soon slowed down, the overstrained and over-tired German infantry could not ensure that von Kleist's supply line would be defended, and a withdrawal was therefore necessary. In late November von Rundstedt ordered such a withdrawal with OKH approval, but the order was immediately countermanded by Hitler. Von Rundstedt thereupon asked to be relieved of his command and was replaced by von Reichenau. The latter, however, despite his earlier fighting talk, came to the same conclusion as von Rundstedt; this time Hitler agreed. However, the Führer decided to assert himself by stipulating that von Kleist should not withdraw all the way to the River Mius, as had been intended. The result was chaos, as von Kleist's mechanized forces (by now with horses replacing many of their vehicles) changed their positions in conformity with Hitler's wishes and then, when the impractical reality of their new position became apparent, were allowed to fall back on the natural line of the Mius. Despite this interlude, however, the move back from Rostov was a smooth operation, but this smoothness could not conceal the reality that for the first time the Red Army had been able to plan and execute a maneuver which forced the Germans to make a significant retreat.

With their lengthy supply lines, the Germans were very vulnerable to partisan activity. However, the

Above: December 1941 on the Soviet West Front. Captured German equipment is studied by Red officers. Second from the left is General Rokossovsky, recently released from a Soviet prison camp.

importance of this in the first year of the war, and indeed throughout the war, has been rather exaggerated in Soviet accounts. The unpreparedness of the authorities is the most evident fact about the early partisan organization. In the earlier 1930s, inspired perhaps by the legendary work of Red partisans during the Civil War, several Soviet generals had developed the techniques of such warfare. In particular, the use of radio and aircraft to maintain touch with (and control over) partisan units had been studied, and the problem of training men to use captured foreign weapons was among other relevant issues that were discussed. But the ascendancy of Stalin, and the execution of that generation of generals which had interested itself in this work, meant the end of this endeavor. Stalin's insistence that in a future war the Red Army would immediately advance into enemy territory meant that anyone who mentioned partisan warfare was, in effect, questioning Stalin's judgment that there would be no Soviet territory occupied by the enemy.

So, when war came, the USSR was unprepared in this field too. In the first desperate weeks the best that could be done was to reprint and issue an obsolete Civil War service paper about how to organize partisan activities. This unpreparedness remains one of those touchy issues about which discussion is still restricted. In accordance with the tendency for such delicate matters to be raised first, and obliquely, in novels, a massive and successful novel of 1945, *The Young Guard* by Fadayev, described how a group of young Communists, unable to find a partisan organization when their native Donets region was overrun by the invader, decided to create their own. This novel won a Stalin Prize before the critics realized that it implied, among other things, that the Red Army retreat was not a planned withdrawal and that the possibility of partisan warfare had been neglected. The unfortunate author had then to produce a revised edition (and later a revised revised edition) to correct these indiscreet implications.

Most of what passed for partisan activity in 1941 was the work of scattered Red Army detachments which had been cut off by the rapid German advance

and had escaped the following infantry, typically by disappearing into the forests. This was one of the disadvantages of the blitzkrieg type of war, with the front line being advanced before its rear could be properly mopped up. Many such detachments eventually fought their way back to their own side of the line, where the welcome staged by the local NKVD units was not always in the best of taste. Other men, especially those who had lost or jettisoned their arms or uniforms, and rightly surmized that these personal losses would be regarded by the NKVD as sure signs of cowardly or traitorous attitudes, preferred to lie low, often joining the true partisans later. Others tried to disappear inside occupied territory, settling in one village or another and eventually being executed when the Red Army advance caught up with them.

1942 was the year in which true partisan activity developed. Lessons of the early 1930s were quickly re-studied, and the Red Air Force arranged an effective network of communications by light aircraft. Later, radio became more plentiful. Radio

Left: The first public execution by the Germans in Minsk, 1941.
Below: Soviet partisans lay a charge beneath a rail; for partisans railway sabotage was a profitable and relatively risk-free activity.

Above: General Belov's cavalry make a traditional attack on a German-held village. The Germans were able to hold out against the Soviet winter offensive of 1941-42 by retreating to fortified poitions in the towns and villages which the Russians had too few reserves and heavy weapons to capture.
Above right: Civilian hostages hung by the Germans at Volokolamsk.
Right: A knocked-out Mark III tank and one of its unfortunate crew on the approaches to Moscow.

operators, as well as other skilled technicians (typically explosives experts, but also including commissars and NKVD personnel) were also landed in partisan-held areas. As in other countries occupied by the Germans, the main target of partisans was not the invaders, but the local inhabitants. This was especially true in the initial period, when it was considered essential to prevent local populations settling down to pursue their normal lives. Murders, often accompanied by mutilation and torture, were used to discourage local inhabitants cooperating with the Germans. Attacks on Germans were made not so much with the aim of reducing the German strength, but of provoking the occupiers to reprisals against the local inhabitants, thereby arousing the latter. The Germans, and especially their security troops, were predisposed to fall into this trap, and their reprisals were savage and unjust, with innocent locals being hung by the hundred. Thus the Germans and the partisans jointly made life unbearable for the villagers, who often took to the forests simply to escape and there found themselves in partisan territory, where they were soon made to realize that joining the partisans, dangerous though it was, offered the best chance of survival.

Initially, the partisans attacked the softest of targets. It was quite early in the war when the

German command realized that single ambulances could not be used to carry wounded back home, because they were very liable to be attacked en route and their occupants murdered. Later, despatch riders became vulnerable; a wire stretched across a road at night killed quite a few of these. But the main significance of partisan warfare as it developed after 1941 was its effect in occupying the attention of German forces which could have been better employed elsewhere, and its threat to supply lines. The work of the German railway troops was sharply criticized after the first few months, and the direction of the railways was taken out of the hands of the military and put under German civilian railway administrators. But probably it was circumstances rather than poor management which were responsible for the near-breakdown of rail communications. The problems of the different gauge, the withdrawal by the retreating Russians of most of the better locomotives and rolling stock, the problems caused by the winter, when water supplies froze up and locomotives could suffer cracked pipes and cylinders, were difficulties enough, and the demolition by partisans of the running lines was in many cases the final blow which could close a railway section for a day or two. Placing and detonating a small charge beneath a rail joint was an easy task where, more often than not, the line ran through forest; just one man could do the job in a few minutes, and then disappear. When partisans became more sophisticated, they could additionally arrange an ambush of the first train to be stopped by the damage, and perhaps of the repair train which was usually the first reaction of the German railway authorities.

Nazi policy in the occupied areas was characterized by a savage arrogance which, instead of taking advantage of the USSR's social and political weaknesses, actually helped to remedy them. Hitler was well aware that the USSR was a collection of nations, most of which to some degree resented the dominance of the Great Russians (Muscovites). Ukrainians, Belorussians and Georgians were among those nations which would have preferred to break away from Moscow to form their own states. This was even more the case in the former Baltic republics of Lithuania, Latvia and Estonia, which had enjoyed their independence until the Red Army took over in 1940. On to this division by nationality there was superimposed a widespread political dissidence, based on hatred or at least resentment of the communist system as imposed by Stalin. On top of these two major divisions were others, of which the conflict between Christianity and communist atheism was probably the most important.

It is said that former tsarist army officers, emigrés in Germany, had advised that all Russians, even including commissars and party members, should be treated gently by the German invaders; in this way the underlying divisions of the Soviet state would soon make themselves felt. The way in which local populations, often led by their village priest, welcomed the Germans, would seem to confirm this. However, Hitler's ideology could not admit such an attitude. On the one hand his expectation of a rapid victory made a contribution toward victory by the USSR's dissident citizens irrelevant. On the other hand Hitler already had strong views on how the

Russians should be treated. The directive about the immediate execution of captured commissars and Jews came in May 1941, before the campaign started. A few months later, in victorious August, Hitler told a conference that in Russia the German task was 'first master, second administer, third exploit'. There followed other decrees, even more irrational; in September a decree provided that for every German soldier shot in occupied territory up to one hundred 'communists' were to be executed in reprisal. In 1942 similar reprisals were authorized against the families of saboteurs, and there were others. Hitler had no wish to capture the hearts and minds of the inhabitants, who in any case were scorned as being of an inferior race.

Although the area immediately behind the combat zone was administered by military commandants, most of the occupied territory was under the German Ministry of the Occupied Territories, headed by Rosenberg. Rosenberg, as a Baltic German, had in fact been born in tsarist Russia, and in several ways he had a better understanding of Russia than did his fellow Nazis; but he, too, was so dominated by ideology that his superior knowledge was hardly utilized. His Ministry changed its mind several times, and its policies were a mixture of confused priorities and contradictory plans. Initially the intention was to accelerate the disintegration of the USSR by establishing new, separate states for the Ukraine, the Caucasus, and other regions or nationalities. But Hitler's desire above all for the subjugation of the inhabitants and the taking for German benefit of all economic resources, soon ended this idea. Soon the concept of *Reich* territories was generally accepted, this implying that eventually the conquered areas would be settled by militarized colonies and fortified farms as a preliminary to eventual peaceful German settlement. Rosenberg was strongly anti-Christian, so any idea of exploiting the religious fervor of the majority of the local populations, with the Germans

Below: Inadequately clad German infantry surrender during the first winter of the Eastern Front campaign. Almost all German prisoners of war died in captivity, as did millions of Russian prisoners taken by the Germans.

Above: Siberian troops defending Moscow with heavy artillery. *Right:* A line of BT-7 light tanks passes down Gorky street in Moscow in a scene from a Soviet propaganda film. The BT-7 tank was armed with a 45mm gun.

posing as Christian soldiers smiting the communist Antichrist, was out of the question.

Below Rosenberg there were two *Reich* commissioners, Koch being in charge of the Ukraine and Lohse of the Baltic states and Belorussia (jointly known by the Germans as *Ostland*). Koch, in particular, was cruel and rapacious enough to discourage any burgeoning pro-German sentiment. The idea of putting an end to the highly unpopular collective farms, which had been bloodily imposed by Stalin, and returning to small family farms, was regarded by several German administrators as a sure way of gaining local cooperation. Some steps were indeed taken in this direction, but Koch put an end to this. He argued that large-scale collective farms made it much easier to take away farm produce from unwilling peasants; ironically, though not perhaps surprising in view of the natures of the Nazi and Stalinist régimes, this was precisely why Stalin had undertaken collectivization in the first place.

Because German army officers, before the war started, had been regarded as unsuitable (because too soft) to carry out the more sordid acts of cruelty which were envisaged, it had been arranged that the SS would be responsible for police, security, and anti-partisan activities. The armed SS formations which originally were intended to fight alongside regular army units were increasingly used in these tasks, to reinforce the Security Service (SD) of Heydrich. It was the SD which, among other things, was responsible for the execution of commissars and Jews.

Thus a given area might be under dual administration by Rosenberg's ministry and by the SD. Rosenberg's civilian administrators, thanks to their bright brown uniforms and their arrogant way of walking around, were nicknamed 'golden pheasants' by the local peasantry, and something less polite by the SD men. Both the SD and the Rosenberg men had to suffer a third layer of administration superimposed on their area. This was composed of officials of the German foreign service, whose activities were sometimes mysterious, partly because they were often directed towards looting for personal, rather than state, ends.

In these circumstances, with Hitler regarding Russians as mere 'swamp-dwellers', it is hardly surprising that little use was made of the non-Russian Soviet units which deserted to the Germans. Many cossack units were among these. In the Ukraine, a nationalist organization soon appeared, ready to fight on the German side, but it was soon repelled by the brutalities inflicted by Koch and also by hurt feelings on account of German policies (notably the transfer to Rumania of Ukrainian territory which included the city of Odessa). In the end the Ukrainian nationalists were fighting both Russians and Germans; among their murder victims was the Russian General Vatutin, and their anti-Soviet activities continued for several years after 1945.

The enormous numbers of Russian prisoners of war took the Germans by surprise, it has been said. Since the capture of so many men was the basic endeavor of the *Barbarossa* Plan this seems to be little more than an excuse to explain why so many hundreds of thousands of prisoners died in the weeks following their capture. The survivors were eventually isolated in camps, either on former Soviet territory or in Germany itself, where they formed part of the Nazi war machine's labor army. To these deportees were added thousands of Russian civilians, rounded up by recruitment organizations and sent to work in German factories. Ill-fed, ill-housed, and overworked, the survival rate of these unfortunates was very low.

It is possible, just possible, that had Hitler taken advantage of the dislike of so many Soviet citizens for the Stalinist regime and the dominance of Muscovite Russians, he might have won this war. Not for the first time he had chosen to ignore Clausewitz, who in the previous century had propounded that Russia was such an enormous country that the only way the Russian government could be overthrown was from within.

Below: Soviet infantry recapture a town near Kaluga during the 1941-42 winter offensive.

In late February 1942 the Russian counteroffensive finally lost impetus and the whole front settled down into a period of recuperation until the opening of the campaigning season expected in May. By early April, not without sometimes acrimonious arguments from his generals, Hitler had decided on a plan for 1942, designed either to end the war or at least allow the Eastern Front to be stabilized behind a strong German fortified line; Germany would then be ready to turn most of its forces toward the west to renew the struggle with Britain which, this time, would also mean fighting Americans.

Neither Moscow nor Leningrad was to be the main objective of this campaign. Moscow was regarded as attainable, but only at the cost of diverting energy from the objectives Hitler considered more urgent. As for Leningrad, the position there was somewhat depressing, although efforts were to continue. During the winter the forward positions to the east of that city had been abandoned, including the important town of Tikhvin. Leningrad had

never been completely cut off; the Germans were disappointed at the Finnish lack of drive, once the Finnish territory lost in the 1939–40 war had been recovered. General von Leeb had resigned when Hitler refused to allow him to withdraw, and as a result of that refusal a substantial German formation was surrounded around Demyansk, south of Lake Ilmen. This in fact was a result of the war's first large-scale envelopment movement by the Red Army, but in the end it did not result in a disaster for the Germans. Absence of effective Soviet fighter squadrons allowed the Luftwaffe to send in waves of unescorted transport aircraft to supply the surrounded forces until circumstances allowed a breakout later in the year. It was found that the Junkers 52 transports, with their weak machine gun armaments, were able to hold off stray Soviet fighters so long as they moved in tight formations, but losses from ground fire were quite heavy.

The main German effort was to be in the south. Hitler was still tantalized by the prospect of capturing the Caucasian oilfields. His own stocks of oil had run perilously low, and he believed that the loss of Caucasian oil would be a death blow to the Soviet forces. Strategically, as his generals told him more than once, the main danger of a thrust to the Caucasus was the long supply route which this entailed. Not only might Soviet forces moving from the north interfere with supplies, but such forces might, if they could concentrate near Rostov, actually cut off the Germans fighting in the Caucasus. However, there was general agreement that the Caucasian objective was attainable.

But Hitler was not content with this. He also wanted to advance to the Volga and take Stalingrad. This city was not of such crucial strategic significance as Hitler claimed. True, a German presence there would cut the important Volga traffic artery (along which moved Caucasian oil products in high-capacity barges). But the Volga would be frozen for half the year in any case. There was a much better

Previous page: At the height of the Russian winter horse transport was sometimes the only practicable transport.
Below: German ski troops pass a Dornier 17P bomber on a Russian airfield.
Bottom: Well-equipped Soviet infantry of the South-West Front assemble for an attack in 1942.

case to be made for directing a Volga thrust not against Stalingrad, but against Saratov, which was an important railroad junction, and for that reason vital to the Soviet war effort; the USSR relied almost entirely on the railroads for the movement of troops and munitions. But whatever the merits of the drive to the Volga, what seemed certain to most of the leading German generals was that a division of forces between the Caucasus and the Volga would most likely mean that neither offensive could succeed. In this they were quite right, as a few months fighting would demonstrate. Hitler, however, seemed to grow ever more confident of his military talent even as his irrationality became more obvious to others. This 1942 Operation *Blau* was imposed against the misgivings of his best advisors.

In preparation, it was planned to split Army Group South into two new Army Groups: Army Group A, commanded by Field Marshal List, with von Kleist's First Panzer Army, was entrusted with the conquest of the Caucasus, via Taganrog and Rostov. It would be covered to the north by Army Group B under Field Marshal von Bock, with Hoth's Fourth Panzer Army. It was to achieve its covering purpose by occupying the Stalingrad area, moving from the south of Kursk and curving south-eastward after by-passing Voronezh. Behind the German armor and infantry on both lines of advance would follow the non-German forces, by now forming a more substantial proportion of the available strength but with a morale and fighting spirit no better than in 1941. The Rumanians, with their 22 divisions, were the strongest element of these but, having gained Odessa after a lengthy siege, they were becoming less keen on further advances. Other divisions were provided by the Hungarians and Italians who, on the Eastern Front as a whole, contributed 10 divisions each. There were also single Spanish and Slovakian divisions, while far to the north the Finns had contributed 17 very battleworthy divisions to the pursuit of their own quarrel with the Russians.

Top: Italian troops suffer from the bitter Eastern Front weather.
Above: Field Marshal von List (left) and Colonel General von Manstein in 1942. List commanded Army Group A in the summer of 1942 while Manstein led the Eleventh Army in the Crimea in the early part of the year before being transferred north to the Leningrad sector until the Russian counterattack at Stalingrad.
Left: Infantry of the Spanish Blue Division in action.

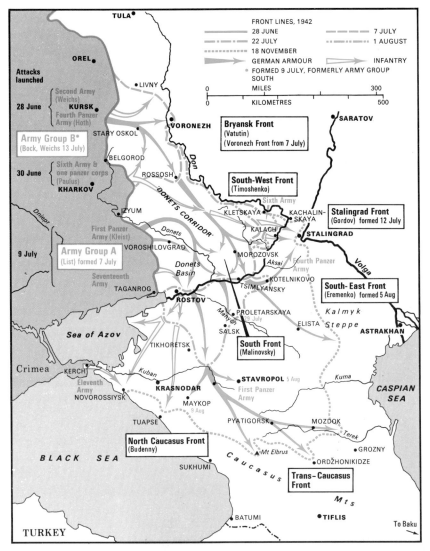

FRONT LINES, 1942
28 JUNE ——— 7 JULY ——
22 JULY —·—·— 1 AUGUST ·····
18 NOVEMBER ·····
GERMAN ARMOUR ➤ INFANTRY ➤
FORMED 9 JULY, FORMERLY ARMY GROUP SOUTH

0 — MILES — 300
0 — KILOMETRES — 500

TULA
OREL
Attacks launched
28 June — Second Army (Weichs) / KURSK / Fourth Panzer Army (Hoth)
Army Group B* (Bock, Weichs 13 July)
30 June — Sixth Army & one panzer corps (Paulus) / KHARKOV
9 July — First Panzer Army (Kleist)
Army Group A (List) formed 7 July
Seventeenth Army
LIVNY
VORONEZH
STARY OSKOL
BELGOROD
ROSSOSH
IZYUM
Dnieper
Donets
DONETS CORRIDOR
VOROSHILOVGRAD
Donets Basin
TAGANROG
ROSTOV
Sea of Azov
Crimea
KERCH
Eleventh Army
NOVOROSSIYSK
Kuban
TIKHORETSK
SALSK
Manych
PROLETARSKAYA 19 July
STAVROPOL 5 Aug
First Panzer Army
KRASNODAR
MAYKOP 9 Aug
TUAPSE
PYATIGORSK
BLACK SEA
SUKHUMI
Caucasus
Mt Elbrus
BATUMI
TURKEY
SARATOV
Bryansk Front (Vatutin) (Voronezh Front from 7 July)
Don
South-West Front (Timoshenko)
Sixth Army
KLETSKAYA
KACHALIN-SKAYA
KALACH
STALINGRAD
Stalingrad Front (Gordov) formed 12 July
MOROZOVSK
Aksai
Fourth Panzer Army
Volga
KOTELNIKOVO
TSIMLYANSKY
South-East Front (Eremenko) formed 5 Aug
Kalmyk Steppe
ELISTA
ASTRAKHAN
Kuma
CASPIAN SEA
South Front (Malinovsky)
North Caucasus Front (Budenny)
MOZDOK
Terek
GROZNY
ORDŽHONIKIDZE
Trans-Caucasus Front
Mts
TIFLIS
To Baku

An important side-campaign in the south was the capture of the Crimea, with the delayed capture of Sevastopol in July. German troops occupied the entire peninsula and thereby provided a shorter route to the Caucasus once the Taman Peninsula was taken. Von Bock, however, was held up for four weeks by a Soviet offensive launched by Timoshenko towards Kharkov in May. The Red troops made initial breakthroughs but soon lost momentum, and the attack ended in another disastrous encirclement near Izyum in late May, with almost a quarter of a million men captured and perhaps 1200 tanks. But, as in 1941, such a great victory obscured the underlying failure, for the thousands of Russian prisoners were no compensation for the loss of weeks which were so precious when the campaigning season was short and distances immense. All the same, since an objective of *Blau* was the destruction of Red troops west of the Don, this success was considered a good augury.

However, the proposed destruction of the Red forces depended not only on what the Germans did, but also on whether the Russians would place themselves in the right positions for further encirclements. The Red generals were now showing some skill in withdrawing just at the right moment, and Timoshenko's mishap would be repeated only if the Soviet high command refused to withdraw its forces across the Volga in good time. On the whole, German encirclement operations were still handicapped by poor intelligence. A weaker Luftwaffe, among other things, was no longer capable of detailed reconnaissance work over long distances. As a consequence, the location of Soviet troop concentrations was often a matter of intuition.

In the first weeks of von Bock's offensive Hitler's interferences caused considerable strains at the front.

Above: The 1942 summer campaign in the south.
Right: The Junkers 52, mainstay of the Luftwaffe transport force.
Opposite: German mountain troops during the fighting in the Caucasus. They are operating an MG 42 machine gun.

Right: Men of a
Luftwaffe airfield
security unit
Below: American-
made Stuart light tanks
near Mozdok in
October 1942.
Center, below; Soviet
naval infantry.
Bottom: German
motor cycle troops in
June 1942.

The Führer decided to capture Voronezh after all, then thought better of it, and finally allowed Bock to make up his own mind; appropriately enough, as the German forces passed by they occupied just a part of that city. More fundamentally, Hitler needled Bock with repeated criticisms that the latter was moving too slowly; Bock justified a slow but steady approach by the need to cover himself against stray Soviet formations operating on his flanks. After passing Voronezh, Bock was reluctant to turn south. Part of his trouble was lack of motor fuel; in the second week of July his Panzer army came to a stop because it had run out of fuel. Thus there was little to prevent the Russians evacuating their forces over the Don,

and the panzers accomplished none of the hoped-for encirclements. Hitler was unconvinced by the evidence presented to him that there were no longer any sizable Red formations on the western side, and continued to press for encirclements of non-existent enemy troops. On 18 July, however, the Führer ordered Army Group B to advance on Stalingrad.

Meanwhile Army Group A was making slow progress in the south. Rostov was captured on 23 July. But List's troops then had to face a trek of over 700 miles if they were to capture the oil center of Baku. En route they would have to cross scores of rivers, then the Caucasian Mountains. Moreover, the withdrawal of many Luftwaffe units to the north and to the African theater meant that only a few Stuka and fighter groups were available. Usually, therefore, the Red Air Force had superiority in the Caucasus. The panzer army's tanks had done considerable mileage and were falling victim to breakdowns, while the mobility of the armored and motorized formations was restricted by a continuous fuel shortage and the occasional fuel crisis. Added to all this, Hitler's orders and directives seemed to alter priorities on almost a daily basis. For a long period the priority seemed to have shifted from the rapid conquest of the oilfields to an equally rapid conquest of the Black Sea coastline, thereby robbing the Red Navy of its remaining bases.

As the German forces moved south, Soviet resistance stiffened, although it was not until the foothills were reached that the Red formations ended their withdrawal phase and began positively to block the Germans. In the end, after more weeks of fighting, during which part of the German strength was transferred to help in the Stalingrad battle, Army Group A had reached most of the Caucasian foothills, and had captured outlying oilfields at Maykop (which, however, had been put out of action by the

retreating Russians). A small party had also climbed Mount Elbrus, Europe's highest mountain, and planted a swastika flag on the summit. Propagandists made much of this, but Hitler was privately infuriated that time was spent on such trivialities while the main issues still hung in the balance. Baku was still hundreds of miles away, and there seemed little prospect of overcoming stiffening Soviet resistance until more forces could be allocated to this theater. So in November, when the first snow fell to mark the end of the campaigning season, von Kleist and his depleted armor were just outside Ordzhonikidze, destined to be the most southerly point reached by the Germans, but a long way north of the main oilfields.

The shortages suffered by the German armies were due partly to transport difficulties, partly to the policy of limiting weapon and munition production to the requirements of short campaigns, and partly to Germany's raw material disadvantages. The Red forces had their own problems of shortages. Transport was certainly a factor in these, but it was the speed and depth of the invasion which was the main cause. The regions occupied by the Germans were those which contained most of the Soviet industrial plant, not to speak of the agricultural resources needed to feed the enormous armies as well as the whole population.

The evacuation of so many Soviet industries in the face of the advancing Germans has been described as a near-miracle and a textbook example of what can be achieved by a plan-conscious, authoritarian regime. There is some truth in these claims, but reality was a little more complex. Firstly, despite the Soviet addiction to planning, the evacuation process was a last-minute expedient, not planned in advance. Secondly, although an amazing quantity of plant was carried east, still more was left behind. All the same,

Top A Soviet woman sniper. The Soviets employed female personnel in a number of combat roles.
Above: German artillery observers installed in a knocked-out Soviet tank.
Left: Infantry of the Totenkopf SS Division. As the war proceeded SS troops made up an increasing proportion of the German forces.

the evacuation was a triumph of improvisation and, often, self-sacrifice. Most of the glory was owed to the railways and railwaymen, and to the workers of the factories involved, whose physical labor was prodigious.

An evacuation committee had been set up in the early days. An initial decision, taken as early as 5 July 1941, was to evacuate all the aircraft factories (three quarters of aircraft production was in the central region of European Russia). Later other factories were removed. Some large plants needed over a hundred freight trains to carry them east, but the average factory needed less than ten. The speed of the Red Army withdrawal was a determining factor; in part of the Donets Basin the German advance was so rapid that most plant had to be left behind. There were, too, some bad decisions. In one region the Party authorities decided to give priority in evacuation to women and children, an untypical concession to sentiment which meant the use of scarce train capacity to carry passengers of no value to the war economy. Elsewhere, on several occasions the military leadership delayed the evacuation of munitions and arms factories until it was too late because it felt it could not afford the loss of production which would occur as soon as the workers began to pack up their plant. There were many cases when the hard-pressed railways could not present the required number of freight trains to pick up factories all ready to move. An effort was made to transport skilled workers, and on average about one third of factory workers were moved with their plant. With trains proceeding nose to tail, often under bombing attack, progress was slow, and it took weeks to reach the Volga area, or beyond, where the factories were

to establish themselves. Resettlement was in the hands of the Party organizations in the receiving areas, but they had little to offer for accommodation. Often factories were split up en route, and were never reunited until after the end of the war. There were instances where the railroads unloaded large factories simply by dumping the packing cases over a several-mile stretch of railroad line. Sometimes machines would be installed and put into production at the same time as they were being enclosed in new walls and roofs. All this signified a heroic and significant effort, but the immediate result was a catastrophic fall in war output for most products. Due largely to misplaced optimism, shell production dropped catastrophically in late 1941, so that the total output for the last six months was only half the army's requirements. In November aircraft produc-

Opposite: Von Manstein and his staff. *Below:* Red infantry take a rest. The soldier at the right is armed with the rather uncommon Tokarev SVT-40 automatic rifle. His comrades have PPSh submachine guns and a Degtyarev light machine gun. *Bottom* German infantry and armor advance in the Caucasus in the summer of 1942.

tion was about 600 machines, just a quarter of the September production. Typically, a high priority factory, like the Kharkov tank works, restarted production in the east just 10 weeks after setting out.

To some extent, but too late to bridge the gap in 1941, American and British help could be relied on. When Hitler had invaded Russia the British prime minister, Winston Churchill, declared that Britain would regard the USSR as a close ally, a statement which came as a great relief to the Soviet leadership, which actually had believed its propagandists' earlier allegations that the British would have really liked to come to some anti-communist agreement with Hitler. From the supply point of view, much more important was US willingness to supply Russia under a Lend-Lease arrangement. Well before December 1941, when the USA was drawn into the war as a full belligerent, American shipments were on their way to Russia. The western allies were never able, or indeed willing, to supply all that Stalin demanded, but in the course of the war an enormous amount of freight was shipped, often at great peril and often including items which were in short supply in their country of origin. Probably the most important items were over 400,000 motor trucks, which provided the Red Army with the motor transport to make its rapid advances possible in the final years of the war. Some aircraft and about 13,000

Below: Soviet KV-1 heavy tanks move up toward the front line. *Below right:* Factory workers making final adjustments to Model 1938 122mm guns. These were a standard Soviet divisional artillery weapon and could fire a 55-pound shell some 22,750 yards.

Right; Stalin's crony Zhdanov makes an uplifting speech to the troops.

Below: MiG-3 fighters are delivered to the Red Air Force in early 1942. These machines were used mostly as high altitude interceptors.

tanks were also sent, although these were small quantities compared to Soviet production. Motor and aircraft fuel were sent, and sometimes were of vital importance. Locomotives totaling almost 2000 units, together with freight-cars, were also of great benefit. The Red soldier had great cause to be grateful for the tins of Spam which made up a large part of his diet, and also for the high-quality US-made army boots which he received. Other items included important deliveries of machine tools, as well as the occasional frivolity typified by several miles of gold braid required for officers' uniforms. In general, war supplies, as distinct from actual weapons, were the most significant. How suitable the weapons turned out to be in Soviet hands is uncertain. Soviet commentators tended to claim that American tanks and British fighter aircraft were inferior to Russian designs. On the other hand, German accounts of the naval war repeatedly mention the good use made of Boston bombers in Soviet air attacks on sea communications. Apart from liaison officers, a temporary RAF detachment and small naval base parties, the allies did not send servicemen. During the first year of the war Stalin did indicate that he would be glad to receive American and British fighting troops, but nothing came of this.

There were several access routes for supplies sent to Russia. Much of the American material was sent across the Pacific to Vladivostok, and in December 1941, when Japan started war against the USA, it was feared that this traffic might be blocked. But despite Hitler's continued urgings Japan steadfastly refused to make war against the USSR, so all that was required was for the US freighters plying to

Left: One of about 2600 British and Canadian-built Valentine tanks which served with the Red Army. Apart from its reliable engine this design was not highly regarded by the Russians.
Below: A Soviet antitank rifle fitted rather optimistically to an antiaircraft mounting.

Vladivostok to be transferred to the Soviet flag. Probably about one half of western aid to Russia during the war passed this way. More could have been sent, but the long distance from Vladivostok to the fighting fronts, and the limited line capacity of the Trans Siberian Railway, made this inadvisable. Moreover, in the first year of war, at least, it was the Arctic sea route which was most important. This, used by allied ships setting out from British or Icelandic ports, passed to the north of Norway and ended either at Murmansk or Archangel. Of these two ports Murmansk was the closest, and was ice-free all the year. Archangel could be kept open only with icebreakers, but had the advantage, unlike Murmansk, of being outside the effective range of German bombers flying from Finland or Norway. A third route was through Iran, which had been occupied by Russian and British troops in 1941, when the pro-German Teheran government seemed to pose a threat to the Caucasus and the British Middle East. As soon as Japanese naval activity was cleared from the Indian Ocean, freighters could be sent up the Persian Gulf, and their cargoes sent by rail into the Russian Caucasus.

Of these alternative routes the Arctic sea route was by far the most perilous. Initially, Hitler did not understand the significance of this traffic; he was notably obtuse in naval matters. However, during one of his successive alarms about British intentions, he visualized an Allied landing in Norway, and in this way had his attention again drawn to the Arctic convoys, which had hitherto been unmolested. He immediately ordered the remaining German heavy surface ships to concentrate in Norwegian ports, with an appropriate complement of submarines and aircraft. Two of the surface ships, the battleship *Tirpitz* and battlecruiser *Scharnhorst* were eventually sunk by the British, but not before their presence had caused considerable anxiety and, in one case, contributed to the rout of a convoy.

These convoys had a close British escort throughout, with a distant covering force (sometimes including American battleships and cruisers) for part of their trip. The loss of 24 out of 36 ships of convoy PQ.17 to Russia was occasioned by the belief in the British Admiralty that German heavy ships were in a position to attack it. It was accordingly ordered to disperse, and consequently its freighters and tankers lost the benefit of the close escort and fell easy victims to attacking submarines and aircraft. Other

Above: German appeal to local inhabitants; 'Germany routed the Bolsheviks, reconstruction is up to you.'
Above right: Heinkel 111 bomber in southern Russia in the winter of 1942-43.
Right: Red infantry storm a village.
Opposite: A German infantryman armed with an MG 15 light machine gun. Although originally designed as an aircraft gun, this weapon was also used, particularly later in the war, by the German infantry.

Right: Soviet paratroops board a Douglas DC-3. At first supplied by the USA, these aircraft were later built in the USSR.
Below: A Mark III tank is loaded onto a special tank-carrying railroad flatcar.

convoys took losses, but not on the same disastrous scale as PQ.17. At one point Churchill decided to suspend the convoys temporarily until the nights became longer, a decision which angered Stalin.

In general, Stalin could not understand that the western allies were unable to squander the lives of their fighting men in the way to which he was accustomed. The reluctance of the allies, and especially of Britain, to land troops in France, was attributed not to the difficulty of such an enterprise and the consequences if it failed, but to a western desire to let Russia exhaust herself as long as possible. As Soviet casualties were in the millions this resentment was partly understandable. On the other hand the contributions made by the western allies in other theaters were minimized. To call the proposed landings in France a Second Front was itself misleading, for the British had been fighting the Germans in Africa since 1941 and on average about one third of German armed strength was held in readiness to meet a British attack. Although the numbers engaged in Africa were small compared to the Eastern Front, it was to Africa, not Russia, that some of the best weapons and, perhaps, the best men, were sent. The argument about when the Second Front should be established dragged on until 1944, when it was at last successfully undertaken. Until then, the American Spam supplied to the Red Army was sardonically nicknamed 'Second Front' by Red Army men.

Above: A Soviet patrol, West Front, early 1942.
Left: A German self-propelled gun, knocked out by Soviet artillery.
Below left: Political commissar Nikita Khrushchev studies the Stalingrad situation with General Eremenko (seated).

By the end of 1942 the Soviet Union had recovered its poise following the near-collapse of summer 1941. For the most part, Stalin had weeded out the least effective generals. Even his crony Budenny had been put in an appointment where he could do little harm. Timoshenko, who had achieved much but had unexceptional ability, was also on his way out. Shaposhnikov, who did have the makings of a great soldier, was too ill to play a great role, but Vasilievsky, who became chief of the general staff, was a man whose intellectual distinction was equal to Shaposhnikov's. The same could not be said of Zhukov, who emerged from the war with the reputation as the Soviet Union's greatest general. Zhukov was a rough-cut man who, if his memoirs are to be believed, did occasionally stand up to Stalin. Perhaps more important, he did have a touch of military talent and also the ability, especially important in Russia, to get things done.

Previous page:
General Rokossovsky, commander of the Don Front during the Soviet Stalingrad counteroffensive.

Above: **Village children collect abandoned German weapons for the Red Army at Stalingrad.**

Stalin, like Hitler, wanted to play the decisive role in directing not only the war effort, but also the day-to-day actions of his forces. But, although he made some very costly mistakes, especially in the first two years, he was on the whole more successful than Hitler. Part of the reason for this was organizational; while Hitler meddled, Stalin commanded. Stalin was the undisputed boss, not least because his generals knew that if he chose he could have them arrested and shot. He also had his own information sources, so that he knew how well his orders were carried out. So whereas Hitler was continually in dispute with his generals, and the latter made a practice of distorting the execution of directives they disliked, Stalin's conferences were characterized by the absence of dissent; discussion of issues might be lively, but as soon as it was clear which side of the argument Stalin had chosen, discussion ceased, and Stalin's view became policy. This practice was near-

Below, main picture:
Soviet T-34 tanks and infantry on the attack on the outskirts of Stalingrad.

Above: A German 15cm Nebelwerfer ten-barrel rocket launcher mounted on a half-track.

fatal in 1941 and 1942, when Stalin's refusal to permit timely withdrawals resulted in colossal encirclements and the loss of about three million men; nor was it particularly helpful in the later years, when Stalin's preference for rapid rather than steady advances meant, again, excessive casualties. All the same, Stalin provided leadership, whereas Hitler provided interference. Neither Hitler nor Stalin had any kind of military education, apart from untrustworthy memories of their own participation in earlier wars. Both, therefore, had little understanding of what was practicable. But Stalin made a habit of listening carefully before deciding while Hitler too often began the examination of a question with his mind already made up, often swayed by his ideology or by his intuition.

Hitler formally took over the function of supreme commander quite early in the Russian campaign, and Stalin occupied that role right from the start. But Stalin had several formal bodies to help him with advice and to work out his proposals. There was a State Committee of Defense, consisting of a selected handful of Politburo members (of whom Beria, head of the NKVD, was one). This decided broad questions of strategy: military, political and economic.

In this field Stalin was undoubtedly both master and masterful, having an inborn ability to see a situation as a whole. For the day-to-day running of operations there was the *Stavka*. This had a fluctuating membership, but Stalin was the chairman, supported by his party colleague Molotov; Voroshilov and Budenny, the Party military specialists, were initial members. Shaposhnikov and Zhukov were also prominent members, while Kuznetsov, commanding the Red Navy, had a permanent place. The *Stavka* had a stock of officers who either attended its meetings or were sent out on its behalf to organize or report on various operations. Zhukov himself was often sent out to supervise an especially critical part of the front and so, later, was Vasilievsky. The peacetime Defense Commissariat still existed, although Timoshenko had given up his appointment as Commissar of Defense to Stalin. The Commissariat's general staff and its branch specialists were, however, transferred to serve the *Stavka*.

On the whole the Soviet command organization was superior to the German. Hitler's supreme headquarters (OKW) and army headquarters (OKH) arrangement, and its trimmings, seemed to be designed to create splits in the military leadership

Left: Hungarian troops man an antiaircraft machine gun.
Opposite Bulgarian infantry at a machine gun post. In early 1942 the Germans were reinforced by some 50 divisions supplied by their assorted allies. These units proved less than reliable, however, in the fiercest fighting.

which Hitler could exploit to get what he wanted, but there was little of this in the Soviet system; Stalin had better methods of getting his own way. Thus, for example, the *Stavka* was a joint services body, with full naval representation and a voice for the air force, whereas OKH was a purely army organization, which, nevertheless, conducted the eastern campaign while OKW looked after the other theaters.

Hitler, however, did not kill his generals, except when they plotted against him. He did at one critical point imprison a formation commander (Heim) who had obeyed his superior's order to withdraw at a time when Hitler had forbidden any retreat, and similar arrests were numerous in the final year of war. Throughout the war a succession of gifted generals who could not stomach his interference and wrongheaded directives offered their resignations, which were accepted. This meant that, on the whole, more pliant generals came to the top, whereas those who had minds of their own tended to disappear as the war progressed, although many were reappointed. On the Russian side this tendency was perhaps reversed. Stalin got rid of his best generals well before the war started. As the war progressed he promoted to positions of responsibility those who seemed to do well, including some who, like the distinguished Rokossovsky, had been released from prison camps. In the early stage of the war he had a number of generals executed, however, and others committed suicide, after they had met catastrophies for which Stalin had been mainly responsible. This was a waste of talent and, together with the pre-war purges, helped to ensure that there were no generals of genius and few of real distinction available to lead the Red Army. But there was a pool of competent generals, and that is possibly what Stalin preferred. Several sources agree that Stalin regarded with some wariness any general who showed signs of an excess of excellence.

Below: Soviet infantry overrun a German bomber base near Stalingrad.

There is little doubt that Stalin worked hard at this war. Each day he spoke by telephone to his front commanders, who were required to report in detail what had happened in the previous twenty-four hours. He studied his maps for hours, discussing this or that proposal with the *Stavka* or representatives of the general staff. In the early months, partly because of signal difficulties but largely because of physical fear, generals often failed to report bad news, but Stalin was quick to spot this. He had his own sources of information, via the NKVD, and was often more rapidly informed of events than the general staff and members of the *Stavka*. On the other hand, true to his usual practice, he did not believe his commanders should have more information than they needed for their own operations. Always secretive, he often concealed important facts even from *Stavka* members. In particular he took responsibility for assembling the Red Army reserves but only released information about the size and location of these reserves when he considered the time had come to use them.

Political commissars were attached to the front commanders, and reported back to Stalin. Many of these, like Khrushchev on the South West Front, stayed with their fronts for long periods. Others were sent out by Stalin with specific short-term objectives. Among them were some insalubrious types, including Mekhlis, whose attachment to a front or an army

Left: General Paulus (second from camera) seen at a command post during the German advance to Stalingrad.
Below, main picture: Stalingrad under siege, a Russian view from the east bank of the Volga. Clearly visible are the riverside bluffs, which gave some protection to the Soviet reinforcements landing on the west bank.

invariably spelled trouble for its commanders. On the strength of vicious and unsubstantiated reports from men like Mekhlis, several competent commanders lost their appointments.

As several commentators have pointed out, the Wehrmacht was exceptionally competent in the field but this technical excellence was wasted by the irrational conduct of the war by the high command (that is, by Hitler), whereas with the Red Army the reverse was the case, with an excellent high command being hindered by the inability of the field formations to undertake any but the simplest operations; any complexity of plan invited disaster. So right up to the end of the war the massed frontal attack was the typical Soviet method, with reliance on weight of numbers having its due effect after repeated assaults. Numerous German eyewitnesses reported how tight formations of Red soldiers, vodka-primed, would march shoulder to shoulder against strongpoints, cheering and singing until they were cut down by machine guns. Not surprisingly, the Soviet casualty rate was very high, killed or missing from 1941 to 1945 totaling between seven and ten million (compared to German Eastern Front losses of about half that figure). Soviet novelists (as opposed to historians, who tend to evade awkward topics) have sometimes hinted why losses were so high. In his 1944 prize-winning novel *Days and Nights*, about Stalingrad, Konstantin Simonov portrays, as a subsidiary character, an officer who orders one suicidal frontal assault after another. Similar characters appear in other novels, although the authors take care to indicate that these officers are punished in the end. In a later novel, *Men Are Not Born Soldiers*, published when Stalin was out of favor, Simonov implies that these mediocre life-squandering officers owed their position to generals who themselves were mediocre and owed their appointments to Stalin, who preferred mediocrities. In this novel there is also an incident in which a commander is removed because his plan of attack,

Above: German heavy artillery fires at Red Army assembly positions.
Right: Remains of a Me Bf 109 fighter brought down over Stalingrad.

although likely to gain a bloodless victory, would not capture a key objective in time for the Red Army Day celebrations.

Apart from the occasional issue of vodka, and the exhortations of their officers and commissars, Red Army men could typically rely on their own stolidity to carry them into hopeless assaults. But perhaps most persuasive of all inducements was the ever-present NKVD. This, the Commissarist for Internal Affairs, had its operatives everywhere and, moreover, possessed its own army which in 1941 comprised about 200,000 men, including armored units.

Although the ultimate purpose of this army was the maintenance of the regime in a possible crisis, its main strength was contained in the frontier guards. These, for the most part, fought bravely on 22 June 1941, but to little effect. Also important were the detachments known as the 'Death to Spies' service, of which the Russian acronym was SMERSH. The main activity of these detachments was the shooting of Russian soldiers, although captured Germans also received a share of their bullets. Red Army units about to begin a perilous attack, or whose men were thought to be unsteady, would be hemmed in at their rear by these NKVD soldiers who, armed with submachine guns, made it safer to go forward than to go back. In the days of retreat in 1941 it was NKVD squads which picked out soldiers and, after a cursory trial, executed them for cowardice or treachery.

Covert NKVD operatives formed a network of informers throughout the army. As in civilian institutions, the local NKVD officer was inevitably known to the army officers among whom he mixed, even though he wore the same uniform. But they did not know which men in their unit were informers working on behalf of the NKVD and controled by the local NKVD officer. Information from informers was passed to a unit's NKVD chief, who might send

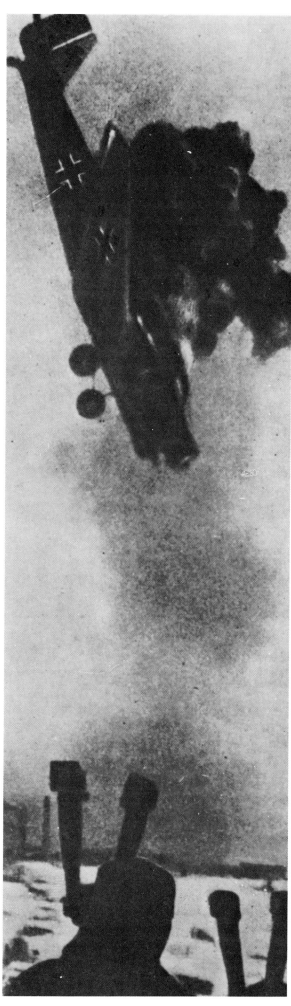

Left: One of the many Junkers 52 transport aircraft which met an end in the unavailing Stalingrad airlift.
Second left: A German-built timber bridge replaces one span of a demolished bridge over a Russian river.

it on in one form or another. Important information went right to the NKVD center in Moscow, and hence to Beria and Stalin's secretariat.

Another incentive to good military conduct were the so-called penal units. These were composed of men who had behaved badly, but not badly enough to warrant execution. The penal battalions were used for sacrificial enterprises; it was these which were used by preference when it was decided to clear a way for assault troops by marching men through enemy minefields. As was only to be expected, many of the NKVD's victims were guilty of nothing; many were arrested on the strength of the anonymous denunciations which secret-police regimes by nature encourage.

However, Soviet society was never all stick and no carrot. At the other extreme from the penal battalions were the Guards units. These, an old tsarist form of discrimination, were units which had distinguished themselves in battle and were granted this elite status which, among other things, brought increased pay and, sometimes, better rations.

In 1942 two measures of some importance were taken. The old regulation that only written orders could be considered valid was relaxed so that at battalion level, and below, oral orders could be used. This regulation, coupled with the general atmosphere

Right: The Nazi flag flies over a captured official building in Stalingrad. In many of the major buildings and factory areas of Stalingrad the Germans had to fight from room to room and floor to floor in their efforts to take the city. *Below:* German troops watch air operations over Stalingrad. Because the fighting in the city was at such close quarters the German close support aircraft were not able to intervene successfully despite German air superiority.

of fear which pervaded the Red Army as a result of the purges and NKVD activity, had meant that, for example, many bridges had been captured intact by the Germans because the officer in charge of the Soviet demolition squad had not received orders to press his button (often because the next superior officer was awaiting instructions from his own superior officer). Also the role of the unit political commissar was again modified. It was clear that effective clear-cut command was now imperative, and for this reason the commissars were renamed 'deputy commanders for political affairs', this making it clear that the unit commander was in full charge.

The Soviet victory at Stalingrad was both a result of the Red Army's recovery and, by boosting morale, a stimulant to a continued recovery. It was not the turning point of the war in a military sense; although it seemed catastrophic to Germans at the time, the actual losses were not crippling. However, insofar as this battle marked the point at which the German campaign changed from an offensive to a defensive operation, it was certainly a landmark. It was also the point at which Hitler's errors of judgment became so frequent and costly that they could no longer be regarded as occasional aberrations, but were seen by his generals to be inseparable from his personality. As Halder expressed it in mid-1942, Hitler's leadership consisted of 'a pathological reaction' to events, coupled with a misuse of the command apparatus.

Strictly speaking, the Stalingrad operations lasted seven months, for they were opened in late June when Army Group B under von Bock began to advance eastward from Kursk toward Voronezh. This advance, and a supplementary advance just to the south from Belgorod, made such rapid progress that Hitler became convinced that the Red Army existed only in small scattered detachments and was no longer in a position to resist the invaders. At about the same time the operations of Army Group A

Left: The massed infantry charge, a favorite Soviet tactic, is employed in the Stalingrad offensive.
Below: Men of General Chuikov's 62nd Army, the Stalingrad garrison, fighting in the ruins of the city.

were under way in the south, aimed at capturing Rostov and proceeding to occupy the Caucasus, the initial task being to cross the Don and thereby attack Rostov from two directions. In mid-July Hitler was afflicted with one of his passing anxieties; he began to fear that the First Panzer Army of Army Group A would be insufficient to force the Don crossings. Against strong opposition from the chief of staff, Halder, he therefore diverted Hoth's Fourth Panzer Army from Army Group B's operations to help Army Group A. Hoth at the time was proceeding rapidly toward Stalingrad, and it seems likely that

Below: Soviet infantry fighting in the Red October factory complex, among the most stubbornly defended sectors in Stalingrad.
Bottom: German self-propelled artillery awaits a target.

if he had not been diverted he would have reached that city before the Russians had time to organize its defense. In other words, just as in the previous year Hitler had diverted armor away from Moscow at the moment when that capital seemed vulnerable to a quick assault, so in 1942 did he sacrifice the likelihood of a quick capture of Stalingrad. Hoth did in fact do well lower down the Don, forcing a crossing at Tsimlyanskaya and accelerating the capture of Rostov, but the presence of two panzer armies in close proximity north of Rostov at this time caused great confusion, for which Hitler characteristically blamed his General Staff.

The capture of Rostov opened the way to the Caucasus, where the Red Army began a long retreat. The ultimate failure of the German Army Group A to reach the oilfields was, however, due not so much to the weakness of the local Red forces (which did, however, have to cope with an anti-Russian mutiny by their Kuban Cossacks), as to the weakness of Hitler's leadership and to a shortage of motor fuel. In this theater Hitler could not decide on priorities or, rather, he changed his priorities all too frequently. Also, as the Stalingrad campaign developed, he transferred much of Army Group A's strength northward to Army Group B, an implicit but unadmitted demonstration that the coexistence of two campaign goals, Stalingrad and the Caucasus, was beyond German strength. As a scapegoat List was removed from the command of Army Group A, being replaced by von Kleist, whose Panzer Army

Above: A German infantry mortar position in a Russian village.
Left: Soviet infantry in the Stalingrad defenses. The standard street fighting weapons, the grenade and the submachine gun, are prominent.

was taken over by von Mackensen. But this change could not alter fundamentals. Because of the advances in the south the German line here grew to no less than 1250 miles, every mile of which had to be defended; if the fronts occupied by army groups north and center were added to this, the total front line exceeded 2000 miles. This, plus the length of the supply lines, represented for a country the size of Germany a strategically impossible situation, but Hitler could not or would not see this.

At the beginning of August Hoth's armor was returned to the Stalingrad operation and immediately began to move toward Stalingrad alongside the railroad route from the north Caucasus. It only took two days to reach Kotelnikovo, but stiffening Russian resistance then made it clear that the chance to take Stalingrad by a rapid armored assault was now gone. Meanwhile part of Army Group B's infantry, in the shape of Paulus's Sixth Army, had slowly approached Stalingrad and crossed the River Don at Kalach. It then faced the last stretch, the tongue of land separating the Don from the Volga. It reached the

latter river, just north of Stalingrad, on 23 August and a little later its forces made contact with Hoth at Kotelnikovo, thereby enclosing Stalingrad in a semi-encirclement; that is, Stalingrad was encircled on its landward side but could communicate with its hinterland across the river.

The Volga at Stalingrad is about two miles wide, the city being on the western bank and stretching, in 1942, for about 18 miles from north to south, being long and straggly in its layout. It was not long before the northern suburbs were occupied by the Germans, and in mid-September Hitler ordered Paulus to capture the city by assault. Because of the virtual impossibility of bridging the wide Volga, reduction by storm seemed the only possible course, since supplies sent from across the river would enable the defenders to withstand a long siege indefinitely. In preparation, Paulus established supply dumps in the area between the Don and Volga and here, too, he built his airfields. The problem with the supply dumps was not, however, the choice of their location, but the means by which they should be stocked. Although Stalingrad in peacetime was well-served by river transport, this was impracticable without complete German control of the river. Reliance had therefore to be placed on two single-track railways, one from Novorossiisk and the other

Right and Above:
Scenes from the Battle of Stalingrad showing Soviet infantry in street-fighting operations.
Center right: The aftermath of a German bombing attack.
Opposite: The strain of the fighting shows on the face of a German soldier.

from Rostov, both of which were decrepit and subject to partisan attack.

A Russian counteroffensive from the south or across the river Volga seemed less likely than one from the north, in view of the Russian troubles in the Caucasus theater. However, an attack from the north was quite possible, and covering forces were kept in place to meet this. There was the Third Rumanian Army west of Kletskaya and north of that there was the Eighth Italian Army between Veshenskaya and Pavlovsk, which in turn was covered to the north by the Second Hungarian Army. To guard Paulus's southern flank a Rumanian Army, the Fourth, had been transferred from Army Group A and held the Ergeni Hills near the Volga. The potential weakness of the troops covering the operation in the north-west was realized by Hitler; he had no great faith in the Rumanians and Italians, but he

felt that the expected rapid conquest of Stalingrad would release troops to reinforce them. However, the assault on Stalingrad made slower progress than expected, and to speed matters Hitler actually detached units from the covering formations to take part in the city battle. Halder did not relish this, and told Hitler that the operation should be abandoned. At this, Hitler decided he had had enough of Halder's warnings, and dismissed him as chief of staff, appointing General Zeitzler in his place.

Stalin's determination to hold the city coincided with his staff's plans for a massive Soviet counter-offensive. An impressive array of military and political talent was sent to the Stalingrad area to supervise, among other things, the work of the garrison commander, the rather run-of-the-mill General Chuikov. The new chief of the general staff, Vasilievsky, was sent, and so was Zhukov, just appointed a deputy

Below: **Destined for a slow death; German prisoners of war at Stalingrad.**

defense commissar. Malenkov was there as Stalin's personal representative, while Khrushchev had arrived with the armies that had retired from the Ukraine. The Soviet plan was simply to keep a very small holding force in the city, charged with defending it street by street, house by house, and room by room. While this garrison held the Germans' attention the Red Army's reserves, which had been steadily accumulating, would be assembled for a counterblow against the Germans around Stalingrad, with a second offensive against Army Group Center, intended mainly to prevent that Army Group despatching reinforcements toward Stalingrad.

The German assault began on 15 September, and it took a week for the Germans to reach the center of the city. This, moreover, represented a fairly small penetration, given the size and shape of the city. Towards the end of the month they reached the northern factory district, the location of the armament works, including the Stalingrad tractor and tank factories which so obsessed Hitler. Also, they captured the Mamaev Heights, which commanded the city, but were soon driven off. The street battles continued day and night, with both defenders and attackers becoming exhausted both physically and psychologically.

Hitler thereupon decided to change his tactics. The assault was to be called off and the city razed by bombing and shelling. However, this did not improve matters, because the Red troops continued to defend each heap of rubble. Finally, in mid-November, German units reached the Volga in the southern part of the city. But Soviet resistance, though now weak, was never fully overcome in Stalingrad. Meanwhile, the British had won the battle of El Alamein and German reinforcements which had been reserved for

the Eastern Front were diverted to Africa.

Forewarning of the Russian counteroffensive was delayed because the massed reserves were concealed, in forests, from air reconnaissance. Due to lack of resources, the Luftwaffe's reconnaissance work was very restricted in any case, and the flow of troop trains seems to have gone unnoticed or been ignored. However, in October it was seen that the Russians were establishing bridgeheads along the Don, which would enable their troops rapidly to pour over that obstacle. Rokossovsky's army opened the attack on 19 November, breaking through the Third Rumanian Army and then advancing to Kalach. Then on the 20th Eremenko broke through the Rumanians in the Ergeni Hills in the south on a front broad enough to grasp Kotelnikovo and at the same time link up with Rokossovsky at Kalach. Formally, this meant that the German Sixth was now trapped, although for some time the Red forces were spread so thinly that Paulus, if he had wished, could easily have broken

out. Zeitzler did in fact urge Hitler to order a withdrawal from Stalingrad before it was too late; it seems he would have persuaded Hitler, had not a boastful Göring assured the Führer that the Luftwaffe could keep the Sixth Army supplied. Hitler thereupon ordered Paulus to create a 'hedgehog' at Stalingrad and await relief.

Hitler then created a new army group, Army Group Don, to handle this crisis. To command it he appointed von Manstein and in it were included the armies in the locality, including the Sixth Army and Hoth's panzer army. Manstein was entrusted with the task of re-establishing a continuous front and then completing the conquest of Stalingrad. However, Hitler more or less dictated the plan of attack, involving an advance by Hoth's armor up the Kotelnikovo-Stalingrad railway which would defeat Eremenko and then tackle Rokossovsky while the latter was dealing with an attack by Paulus from the Stalingrad direction. Meanwhile an infantry attack

Right: General Rodimtsev, commander of the 13th Guards Division, talks to a group of his men in November 1942, at the height of the Battle of Stalingrad.
Below: Soviet troops in action with a 76.2mm field gun in the fighting for Stalingrad.

would come in from the west and encircle Rokossovsky after finishing off Eremenko. This was a highly optimistic plan, but within nine days Manstein was within 30 miles of Stalingrad. But at this point he realized that the Russian strength was sufficient to prevent further progress and, in defiance of Hitler's instructions, he invited Paulus to break out while it was still possible. Paulus, unwilling to move without Hitler's authorization, refused. Manstein's forces thereupon retired, threatened by a sweeping offensive to the north by Vatutin's army which had crossed the Don, already frozen, and routed the Italian Eighth Army.

Possibly the success of the Demyansk airlift encouraged Göring in his assurance that he could keep Stalingrad supplied at the rate of 500 tons of freight each day. The Luftwaffe commanders on the scene, including von Richthofen, knew differently and did not conceal their opinions. But despite their protests the airlift was ordered. As commander of Luftflotte 4, Richthofen was responsible for this endeavor. He was instructed to begin with a daily target of 300 tons of fuel and weaponry, which was soon enlarged to include food. This aim proved quite impossible to achieve. Junkers 52 transport aircraft were used from the start, but these had to be supplemented by Heinkel 111 bombers whose cargo capacity, naturally enough, was limited. A few fighters were provided to protect the flights, but these could not prevent losses by ground fire as the planes landed and took off from the Pitomnik airfield outside Stalingrad. Only a proportion of the aircraft was available at any one time; some needed damage repair, while others were affected by the sub-zero

Opposite: A Red soldier waits to be ferried across the Volga to join the Stalingrad garrison. He is armed with an American-made Thompson submachine gun.
Top: German prisoners at Stalingrad.
Above: Soviet infantry close in on the last German positions.
Left: German tanks abandoned and overrun by the Soviet counteroffensive, at the village of Peskovatka near Stalingrad.

Below: Red infantry
fighting around the
Red October factory.
Opposite, top:
Fighting inside the
factory.

Above: The military
council of the 62nd
Army at Stalingrad.
General Chuikov, the
garrison commander,
is second from the left.
Redesignated the 8th
Guards Army, the
formation remained
under Chuikov's
command until the
Battle for Berlin in
1945.
Right: Soviet forces
defend one of the
Stalingrad factories as
Shturmoviks fly
overhead.

temperatures. On the supply airfields maintenance fitters had to work with no cover from the bitter snowstorms, and the aircraft suffered from being parked in the open. Engines often refused to start, and had to be cosseted at all times. Von Paulus complained that he had been promised 600 tons daily, and that even on the best days he received barely 100 tons. In late December a fresh Soviet offensive brought Red units close to the two main supply airfields, but Göring refused to allow the transport aircraft to evacuate. He expected a heroic continuation of the airlift until the last possible moment. At one of the airfields, Tazinskaya, orders to quit were still awaited when Russian artillery opened fire on the runways. The local commanders were reluctant to defy Göring's orders and only at the very last minute did a staff officer arrive with the nerve to order an immediate escape. What ensued was a panic, as about 150 transport aircraft jockeyed for position on the runway. The result was that about one third of them were destroyed, while all the ground equipment, so important for re-establishing the aircraft at another base, was lost. However, within a few days, transport aircraft were again flying to Stalingrad from more distant airfields. Longer trips meant fewer trips, and in addition to this deterioration the receiving airstrips were functioning badly. A fast turnround of aircraft was impossible, as the ground unloading crews, starved and depressed, no longer performed their tasks with any energy. Aircrews meantime had to prevent their aircraft being boarded by German soldiers intent on deserting while they could; on the return flight wounded were carried out, but only a proportion of these could be accommodated, the others awaited their end at Stalingrad, being destined for death inflicted either by the Russians or by the cold.

As a final endeavor, 18 four-engined Condor aircraft were allocated to the airlift. Their ample cargo capacity promised better things, but they soon succumbed to anti-aircraft fire and poor maintenance. A prototype batch of the new four-engined bomber, the Heinkel 177, was also drafted in, but they proved useless for transport purposes. Reconverted to bomber service, these aircraft made a few raids on the Red Army but were found to burst spontaneously into flames without any assistance from the enemy; they were soon nicknamed 'flying fireworks'. In due course Pitomnik airfield was captured by the Russians, and a pitifully small airstrip at Gumrak was used instead. This was under regular artillery fire, but nevertheless the planes continued to land. At Pitomnik the Russians set up decoy landing lights, and several German planes landed and were captured.

This airlift cost the Germans nearly 500 aircraft. Towards the end Hitler removed Göring from control, replacing him with the less flamboyant but very capable Milch. The latter did what he could, but it was a hopeless endeavor. By that stage the flights were of 300 miles, so aircraft had to carry more fuel and less freight. The Germans in Stalingrad, fighting the Russians on the perimeter and Chuikov's men in the city, were short of ammunition, had almost nil rations and no fuel, and were exposed continuously to bitter temperatures. Paulus was invited by the Russians to surrender, and was promised various terms if he did so. However, he refused and on 22

January Rokossovsky began the final attack. That day Paulus hinted in a message to Hitler that it was time to capitulate, but the Führer would not even accept the idea of a break-out by surviving troops in small groups. Von Manstein urged Hitler to allow a capitulation, but Hitler (by this stage probably correctly) argued that continued resistance would be useful whereas a capitulation would bring nothing, not even any hope for the lives of the German prisoners.

On 31 January Hitler promoted Paulus to the rank of field marshal, presumably to encourage him. But that same day a Red detachment penetrated to the Stalingrad city square where, in the cellar of a department store, Paulus had his headquarters. The fledgling field marshal and his staff were taken prisoner, and the last German detachments at Stalingrad surrendered on 2 February.

In this defeat the Germans lost about 200,000 dead and prisoners, and a good deal of equipment (the equivalent of 6 months' production of tanks for example). Few of the prisoners ever went home. Most died from starvation or cold or disease in the first few weeks. The wounded were helped to die by the Russians. In Germany the surrender, long expected by all except those who still believed propaganda, was treated as a national disaster in which great heroism had been shown. Paulus was publicly praised, although in private Hitler bitterly attacked him. Paulus evidently did not think highly of Hitler either, because it was not long before his voice was heard in the USSR urging Germans to get rid of Hitler. After the war, unlike most of his men, he was released by the Russians and returned to East Germany in 1953.

Below: Major General Krylov, chief of staff of the 62nd Army, at Stalingrad in December 1942.

As the pessimists had forecast, the end result of Hitler's grasping for both the Caucasus and Stalingrad simultaneously was that he lost both. At the time of the Stalingrad defeat, Germany had six corps in the Kuban (north Caucasus), and their position was now perilous, because they could be so easily cut off by Soviet advances from the north. Since they had two alternative lines of communication, one through Rostov and the other through the Crimea and across the Kerch Strait to the Taman Peninsula, Stalin decided that the main effort should be made on the Peninsula, which would threaten both routes. An amphibious landing was to coincide with Soviet thrusts toward Krasnodar and Novorossiisk.

Thanks largely to the Russians' habitual lack of caution with their radio transmissions, German intelligence had a fairly accurate knowledge of what

Above: German forces on the retreat in southern Russia in January 1943.
Pages 140-141: A picture celebrating the beginning of the Soviet counteroffensive at Leningrad in January 1943.

Left: Soviet naval landing party comes ashore at Novorossysk in February 1943.
Opposite: German infantry on the defensive in early 1943.

Left: Soviet infantry pass a dead German shortly before the recapture of Mozdok by the Trans-Caucasus Front in January 1943.

Below: Map showing the small scale of the German advance against the Kursk salient and the subsequent Soviet counterattacks.

was about to happen. This helped to ensure that the main amphibious landing at Novorossiisk was a costly fiasco. However, a secondary landing which had been designed as a feint met with success and was exploited. But although the Russians could assemble enough forces there to prevent its dislodgement, they could not land enough to drive the

surrounding Germans back, the result being a baleful stalemate.

But under Red Army pressure Krasnodar was abandoned, and on 14 February von Manstein quit Rostov, although not before the First Panzer Army had made its escape (the rest of von Kleist's Army Group A took refuge in the Taman Peninsula). Stalin and his *Stavka* then resolved to cut off the retreating Germans further in the rear, on the Dniepr. Hitler, attaching great importance still to the economic possibilities of the occupied territories, was opposed to abandoning the Donets Basin, although von Manstein persuaded him to permit a withdrawal as far as the River Mius. This obstinacy did in fact upset Soviet plans, which had anticipated that the Germans would do what was tactically most wise and withdraw further, to the Donets River. The Russian South West Front was ordered to block a German retreat from the Crimea while at the same time stopping the Germans withdrawing to Zaporozhe and Dnepropetrovsk. Kharkov, meantime, was being encircled by the Red Army, and the SS Panzer Corps which was holding it seemed in peril. Hitler refused to allow it to withdraw. But before the Red Army could thicken the encirclement the Corps, defying Hitler's orders, broke out. Kharkov was lost but the valuable panzers were saved.

The German position on the Mius was held, but was threatened by lack of covering forces to the north. Taking advantage of this, and ordered to make for the Sea of Azov, was the Soviet Sixth Army, with an armored group under Popov in advance. The latter got to within 40 miles of Zaporozhe, but then von Manstein scraped together three panzer corps which, although well below establishment in number of tanks, attacked so vigorously that the Soviet penetration was slowed. Pitched battles ensued in which the Soviet formations were largely destroyed, although most of the Red soldiers, less their heavy equipment, were able to escape. A contributory cause of this Russian setback was a fuel shortage at a crucial point, a shortage well-known to the Germans thanks, once more, to indiscreet Soviet radio messages. In the end, because of von Manstein's unexpected success, the panzer corps which had quit Kharkov in mid-February recaptured that city in mid-March. The next stage would have been to attack the huge salient which the Russians now occupied to the west of Kursk. However, the reluctance of von Kluge to contribute forces to such an attack, and the onset of the thaw before he could be persuaded to change his mind, meant that this operation was postponed to a less propitious time.

Much further north, the Russians improved their position at Leningrad. Thanks to the importance attached in 1942 to Stalingrad and the Caucasus, the German Army Group North had been weakened and was in no position to undertake offensives. Leningrad itself was still under siege, and its inhabitants were dying rapidly from the diseases associated with starvation. All expedients had been exhausted; even wallpaper had been stripped from peoples' apartments so that the paste could be licked off. Although everybody, officially, was entitled to rations, only the rations of children and of those making a contribution to the defenses were large enough to promise continuing life. Although sporadic deliveries were made to the city across Lake

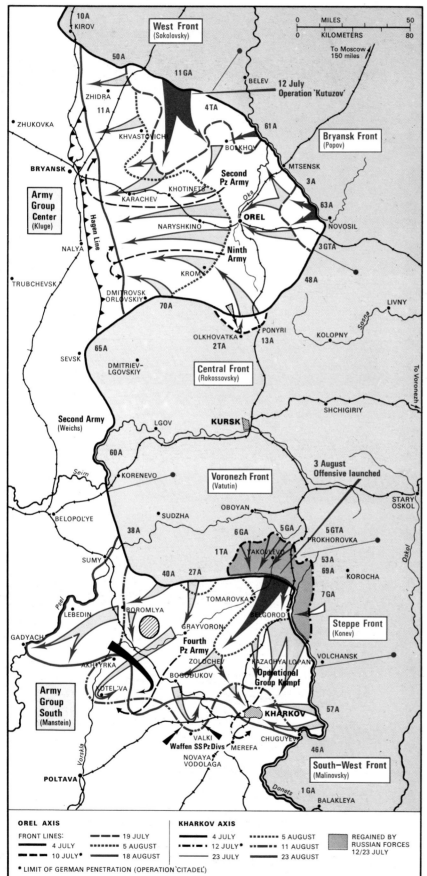

 OREL AXIS

FRONT LINES:
- – – – 19 JULY
- ——— 4 JULY
- – · – 10 JULY *

KHARKOV AXIS
- ——— 4 JULY
- – · – 12 JULY *
- ——— 23 JULY

- · · · · · 5 AUGUST
- · · · · · · 5 AUGUST
- · · · · · · 18 AUGUST

- · · · · · · 5 AUGUST
- – · · – 11 AUGUST
- ——— 23 AUGUST

REGAINED BY RUSSIAN FORCES 12/23 JULY

* LIMIT OF GERMAN PENETRATION (OPERATION 'CITADEL')

Ladoga (where at one stage a railroad was laid across the ice) these were tiny in relation to the volume needed. But in January 1943 the Red Army was able to clear a strip of land along Lake Ladoga and by February railroad men were bringing in supplies along a newly laid line. But, again, a singletrack railroad within the range of German guns could only bring a small alleviation. Efforts by the Red Army to capture the nearby rail center of Mga failed, their attacks being expensively repulsed by, in the main, non-German troops of the Spanish volunteers (the 'Blue Division') and pro-Nazi Dutch and Belgians (the Flanders Legion). South of Leningrad a very successful withdrawal from the Demyansk pocket was made, despite Timoshenko's fierce efforts to close the neck of this pocket. That was in February, and in March, following an unusual period of flexibility in Hitler's attitude, another tactical withdrawal was effected. This resulted in the flattening of the German bulge around Rzhev, thereby eliminating a tactical weakness and also shortening the German line by a very valuable 200 miles.

Thus when the 1942–43 winter campaigning season finished, Germany had suffered several reverses, but had stabilized its positions on a new line and, finally, won a victory at Kharkov over the over-extended and over-optimistically-led Red Army. There were two points about this last-minute success which should have given Hitler pause for thought, but apparently did not. Firstly, von Manstein's victory was largely due to the mustering of mobile reserves, and this had been accomplished by a shortening of the line; the withdrawal from most of the Caucasus and the elimination of the Rzhev salient being important contributions to this. Thus it was evident that further reverses could only be avoided by a reduction of commitments, enabling sufficient forces to be made available in the vital sectors. Secondly, the SS panzer corps which had most distinguished itself in the Kharkov fighting was made up of units that had recently been rested and refurbished; whenever German formations approached their strengths of 1941, they continued to smash corresponding Soviet formations. But by early 1943 almost all German units were well below strength, the combined total of manpower shortfalls in the German units approaching half a million. Although the number of divisions on the Eastern Front was greater than in 1941, the number of men was less. In equipment the situation was even worse; there was one day in January 1943 when the number of tanks available for use on the entire Eastern front fell to less than 500. Losses, but especially long repair periods occasioned by high mileages, heavy usage, and spare parts shortages, accounted for this, together with the inability of German industry to build at a rate sufficient to compensate for losses. Almost 3300 tanks had invaded Russia in 1941, and even that figure had been perilously low in relation to the task.

In the first two years of the eastern campaign the Germans had lost about 8100 tanks. Production of new tanks (and this figure includes assault guns but excludes the lightest tanks) was only 2875 units in 1941, rising to 5500 in 1942, with a rise in output in the next two years thanks to the efforts of Speer, the new armaments minister. Not only was output in the early years insufficient to cover both losses and

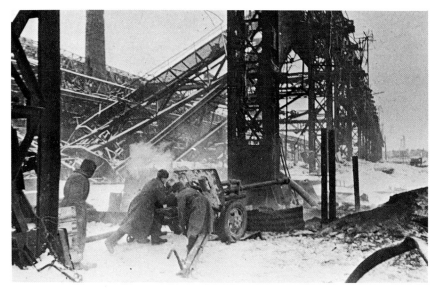

Top: Soviet 76.2mm gun in a street battle.
Above: A German Tiger tank and SS infantrymen rest near a village in the Belgorod area. Most of the area of the Kursk battlefield had similar low rolling hills and occasional small villages.
Left: T-34 tanks on the assembly line. By 1943 Soviet tank production far outstripped the German effort.

Center right: General
Vatutin whose
Voronezh Front bore
the first attacks of the
German southern
pincer in the Battle of
Kursk.
Below right: Marshal
Zhukov at a command
post in 1943.
Below: Marshal
Malinovsky,
commander of the
South-West Front in
1943 flanked by two
other important Soviet
commanders,
Meretskov (left) and
Vasilievsky. The
photograph dates from
1945 when all three
were involved in the
brief war against
Japan.
Bottom: Marshal
Tolbukhin, who led the
Fourth Ukraine Front
in the Soviet
counteroffensive
which followed the
Kursk battle.

repair time, but the types produced were little better than those with which Germany had begun the war. Most of the output was concentrated on improved variations of pre-war designs. True, the new Panther and Tiger tanks were just beginning to enter service at the start of 1943, but the Mark III and the Mark IV still composed the bulk of production. These old models now carried sideplates for protection against projectiles striking their flanks, and their main armor was increased. Most important, their guns had greater muzzle velocity, thanks to a lengthening of their barrels. But these were only palliatives, and did not make these tanks the equal of the Soviet T-34 series. In 1943 the Mark III was finally taken out of production (with a consequent temporary disruption of production lines). The Mark IV was given a more

powerful main gun, still of 75mm but with a longer barrel, giving a nominal penetration capacity of over 6 inches at fairly short ranges instead of the 2 inches of the original gun. The Mark V Panther tank had an even better 75mm main gun than the latest Mark IV, and thicker armor. The Mark VI Tiger heavy tank had an 88mm main gun; though relatively slow and with limited fuel capacity, it was for some time the most powerful tank in the world. Even when the Soviet KV tank was upgunned with an 85mm weapon it was still no match for the Tiger. Only the Russian Iosif Stalin (IS) heavy tank, first used in 1944, could deal confidently with Panthers and Tigers. The IS-2 production model, with 122mm gun, was somewhat lighter than the Tiger but equally well armored; the price paid for this was in

operating convenience, crew comfort, and size of ammunition stock.

German industry also provided self-propelled guns, which could work alongside tanks if necessary. The Red Army received its first batch of Soviet-built self-propelled guns only in December 1942, but by the end of the war they accounted for one third of the total Soviet armored strength. In most types of artillery, however, the Germans were losing their superiority not only in number but also in capability of weapons, and this was despite the inanities of weapon selection which occurred in several instances in the USSR. In the first two years of war the only major improvement in German equipment was the general issue of a 75mm anti-tank gun, which was badly needed to deal with the T-34 tank. By 1943 two characteristic signs of artillery poverty could be seen in the German army: there was an appreciable use of non-German guns, including guns captured from the Soviet, French, Czech and Yugoslav armies, and there was increasing reliance on the 'poor man's gun', the heavy mortar.

The most marked contrast between 1941 and 1943 could be witnessed in motor transport. Although the invasion army had in fact an insufficiency of trucks, it had enough to carry its motorized infantry in their rapid advances. But by 1943 units which were nominally motorized were using horses to a large extent. Units which had entered Russia with their men riding in trucks and their officers in cars, were now withdrawing on foot, with their officers mounted on scrawny horses. And at exactly the same period the Red Army was becoming more mobile; its infantry rode increasingly on trucks and its officers careered around in jeeps. The trucks, like the jeeps,

Left: Panzerfaust antitank weapon in service in the Ukraine in 1943. The weapon shown is the original version with 30m range. This was subsequently increased to 100m.
Bottom left: A young Russian boy shines the boots of German wounded at a station behind the lines.
Below: A Soviet 152mm howitzer in action.

were American, and were better in mud and snow than both the German- and Soviet-built trucks.

The condition of the Luftwaffe had declined even more than that of the army. This was partly because it was heavily engaged with the British, and later American, air forces. Its total losses were serious, and about 60 percent of them were inflicted by the British and Americans. Although total production exceeded total losses (25,000 and 17,500 respectively in 1943), trained and experienced aircrews could not be produced so easily. When a concentrated effort was made, the Luftwaffe could in 1943 still obtain local air superiority on the Eastern Front, but the conditions of 1941, when total air superiority was a fact and ground attack operations could proceed without interference, were no longer enjoyed. By the end of 1943 the Luftwaffe had about two million regular officers and men, although this included men whose functions in other countries were undertaken by the army. The army stood at about five and a quarter million men, of whom, however, nearly two and a half million were outside Russia, dealing with partisans and awaiting attack from the British and Americans, whose control of the sea meant that German strength had to be spread to meet possible attacks from several directions. Hitler expected an Anglo-American invasion long before the western allies were in a position to invade. Because geography implied that their landing would be close to the German frontier, whereas there was plenty of room to maneuver between Germany and the Red Army, the probable western invasion was considered more important than the actual Soviet advance.

Unlike the USSR, Germany had little in reserve. At the time of the Stalingrad disaster it had been decided that Germany should, after all, move over to a war economy, just like Britain had done in 1939. With over seven million young men leaving their occupations for military service between September 1939 and December 1942, an increase of production, which entailed the abandonment of the one-shift operation of factories which had persisted even after two and a half years of war, was difficult, especially as Hitler was resolutely against the idea of German womenfolk soiling their hands in factory work. The labor gap was filled with foreign volunteers, semi-volunteers, and forced labor. But such a workforce, even if properly fed and housed, was not likely to prove an efficient substitute. This problem was never completely solved and it is quite likely that the rather large numbers of German shells and bombs which failed to explode were a consequence of employing hostile workers in munition factories.

The Red Army, with its Air Force, totalled at least six and a half million men in 1943, of which about four million were ground combat troops stationed in the war zones. This six and a half million was about equal to the number of killed and missing which the Soviet forces had lost up to that time. The number of tanks (and self-propelled guns) at the end of the year on the Eastern Front was at least 5500, and aircraft at least 9000.

The Russians had something better than the mortar. This was a truck-mounted multi-rocket projector which could lay a dense pattern of high explosive missiles with demoralizing effect. The Red Army men called it the *Katyusha*, and it was the forerunner of rocket weapons used subsequently by most armies. Production of weapons increased very rapidly after 1941, about 25,000 tanks being produced in each of the two following years. However, it was only in 1943 that the production of the not very useful light tanks ceased, allowing the assembly lines to concentrate on T-34 and KV tanks and the self-propelled guns. Aircraft production in 1943 was about 30,000. Gun production was also at a very high level. In 1944, the last complete year of war, Soviet production would rise to even greater heights (29,000 tanks, 32,000 aircraft, 56,000 field and anti-tank guns). However, German industry by 1944 was beginning to overcome the lag caused by the early reluctance to move to a full war economy. In that year, despite the Anglo-American air bombardment, German industry produced almost 18,000 tanks and self-propelled guns, and over 37,000 aircraft; but despite some successful work with jet propulsion, aircraft designs were little improvement on those of 1939, being mainly modifications of pre-war types, incorporating improved engines and armament. German production had to match both Soviet and Anglo-American production. In 1944, for example, Britain produced 26,000 aircraft and 5000 tanks while American industry manufactured 96,000 aircraft and 17,500 tanks.

Below: SS infantrymen taking part in Operation 'Zitadelle.'

The German failure to crush the Soviet Union, and especially the reverse at Stalingrad, had an unsurprising effect on Germany's relations with her allies and benevolent neutrals. Moreover, fence-sitting governments, like that of Portugal, began to wonder whether it was time to enter the war on the winning side; few now believed that Germany could hope to win the war. Even Germans who heard and saw nothing which had not been approved by the propaganda ministry began to doubt whether Germany could avoid defeat, although as prospects worsened many Germans began to place even more faith in Hitler's ability to find a way out.

Portugal, which was soon to declare war on Germany, at this stage responded to British pressure (and British money) by ending its exports of wolfram (a tungsten compound) to Germany; hitherto this had supplied three quarters of the German demand. For similar reasons German imports of chrome from Turkey almost ceased. In 1943 Sweden also changed course. Hitherto its neutrality had been highly benevolent and had been stretched to permit the passage of German troops across its territory. Sweden also supplied much of Germany's iron ore requirement. But after Stalingrad the Swedish government, although aware that some Swedes had been entranced by Hitler's ideology, decided that skin-deep neutrality was not deep enough, and became less acquiescent. These defections were of great concern to Hitler, who had always been obsessed by Germany's need to import so many of the raw materials necessary for the waging of war.

Equally disturbing were the quarrels that erupted between Germany and its fighting allies. The Finns had always taken an independent course, but hitherto had mainly kept to themselves the belief that they were Germany's allies by chance rather than conviction. They had accepted German help in reconquering those parts of Finland which Russia had taken in 1940, but did not wish to go much further. Moreover, the continuation of this war, which the

Finns had expected to be short, was ruinous for such a small country, and the Finnish government was in urgent need of peace, and after Stalingrad made no secret of this wish.

The greatest animosity was between Rumania and Germany. For this there were several causes, mainly of German origin. When the Russian counteroffensive at Stalingrad broke through the Rumanian covering army and caught the Germans from the flank, Hitler delivered a long reprimand, in person, to the Rumanian leader, Antonescu. Since the Rumanians had sustained heavy casualties, this was not only a blow to the always sensitive Rumanian pride, but was also considered an insult. Having examined the weakened position of Hitler, Antonescu a few days later responded by asking for all Rumanian troops to be withdrawn from the battle areas. Rumanians were also irked by the ever more obvious German intention to squeeze them out of the territory between the Bug and Dniestr, which they had come to regard as theirs by right of conquest. The Hungarians and Rumanians, fighting on adjacent fronts, also were in a state of mutual hostility, largely because Hitler had earlier recommended that Rumanian Transylvania should be returned to Hungary. During the course of 1943 the Hungarian units on the Eastern Front began to ignore the

Above: An assault gun of an SS armored unit crosses the rail tracks at Belgorod with a derelict Russian locomotive in the background.
Left: Infantrymen of a German armored division search for a partisan group.

requests of the German army commanders, and in November the Hungarians additionally demonstrated their dissatisfaction by requesting that their three corps in Russia be kept away from the battle areas. At about the same time Franco requested the return to Spain of his Blue Division, and the Slovakian government, hitherto regarded as a pliant German puppet, also intimated that it was reluctant to see the Slovakian Legion engaged in further fighting. Mussolini, soon to be deposed, recommended that a peace, almost at any price, should be made with Russia, and commenced to withdraw his troops.

To stem this loss of prestige was one reason why Hitler sought a massive victory over the Red Army in summer 1943. Another reason was that this seemed the last year in which Germany, in effect, could fight on two fronts. Although the Anglo-Americans had not yet landed on the continent of Europe the ever-present possibility that they might do so was already causing bitter wrangling in the German high command. The OKW was responsible for the western defenses, while OKH was in charge of the Eastern Front, and each thought it had an obvious claim to reinforcement at the expense of the other. This conflict had a logical basis in that Germany's resources were obviously over-stretched. OKH would only tolerate a reduction of its strength so long as there was a corresponding reduction in its tasks, and notably a shortening of the front. Since a shortening of the front implied a withdrawal, and since such a withdrawal implied the loss of Russian territories which Hitler rightly or wrongly (usually wrongly) considered vital to Germany, there was a stalemate. In a sense the proposed offensive in the east was a temporary solution to the problem. A

sound defeat of the Red Army would permit the Germans to stabilize their defensive line, which they could then hold with fewer men, thereby providing reinforcement for the armies in western Europe. Finally, an additional encouragement was von Manstein's recent victory at Kharkov, which seemed to show that the Germans could still crush the Russians, given the right conditions.

The German plan was named Operation *Zitadelle*, and the ensuing battle is known as the Battle of Kursk, or of the Kursk Salient. Among other things, this battle has entered the textbooks because it was, by several definitions, the biggest tank battle ever known. The German line in south central Russia at this time was marked by a huge westward bulge, this being the Kursk Salient, containing that city among others and being defended by the Soviet Central Front. North and south of this were German salients, the two together resembling a jaw ready to engulf the rather larger Kursk Salient. For the high commands of both sides, this situation clearly gave great opportunities, and both realized there would be a great struggle here; for each the problem was whether to attack first, or to wait until the enemy had begun an attack before moving in to cut off his rear. Hitler's original intention was to start the battle in April, but it was hard to gather enough troops to satisfy the demands of Model, whose Army Group Center would be the main participant.

Plan *Zitadelle* envisaged that the Ninth Army would advance southward from the Orel direction and at Kursk link up with a northward German advance from the Kharkov direction, the latter thrust being undertaken by Hoth's panzer army and the Kempf Group from Army Group South. As in previous German victories the Russians would be

Below: A Soviet reconnaissance in force during the battle for Poltava in September 1943.

caught in an encirclement and progressively destroyed by German infantry. It seemed a good plan, but several of those involved in it seem to have lost their earlier optimism. Model, explicitly by letter and implicitly by demanding more troops, believed that the Russian armies were stronger than alleged, and would therefore win time to call up reserves. Von Kluge and von Manstein lost enthusiasm as the delays mounted for they felt, justifiably as it turned out, that time was not on the German side; the Russians were becoming stronger every day. Guderian, who had been forgiven a past quarrel and invited out of retirement to supervise the armored forces of the entire army, as an inspector-general, did not like the plan at all, because his main object was to amass

tanks for the anticipated Western Front, and Plan *Zitadelle*, successful or unsuccessful, could only hinder him in that task. Von Kluge did not find Guderian's attitude at all admirable (they had a long-standing personal animosity), and challenged him to a duel which did not, however, take place. With all this discussion, and with Hitler apparently not so cocksure as on previous occasions, it was not until 4 July that the offensive was launched. The intervening weeks had enabled heavy artillery and more heavy tanks to be assembled. The latter included a few of the brand new Panther (Mark V) and recently introduced Tiger tanks, as well as the self-propelled anti-tank gun version of the latter, known as the Ferdinand. None of these had been finally accepted

Above: Under artillery cover, Soviet sappers clear minefields in front of a German position.

Left: Abandoned German Mark IV and III tanks in Soviet custody after the Battle of Kursk.

Above: A German
column falls victim to
Soviet air attack in the
fighting at Kursk. As
well as marking the
demise of the German
tank force, the Kursk
battle also saw air
superiority pass from
the Luftwaffe to the
Soviets.

by the German Army, and it was unwise to commit
them to battle at that stage of their development;
presumably the 88mm gun of the Tigers and Ferdinands was their attraction for Hitler, whose decision
it was to use these tanks. On the Eastern Front at
this time there were about 3700 tanks available to the
German Army (including about 1000 self-propelled
guns). About 2500 of this total were allocated to
Operation *Zitadelle*, of which about 2000 were tanks.
About 1000 tanks were at the disposal of von Manstein's thrust from the south, this total including
about 300 Panthers and Tigers. In the north, Model
had almost 1000 tanks. The Luftwaffe provided about
1800 aircraft at the start of the operation.

The strength of the Russians is not precisely
known. What is certain, however, is that the Soviet
command had decided to await the German assault
before launching its own. This meant, among other
things, that great attention had been paid to defensive
fortifications around the Kursk Salient. Close to the
perimeter were five parallel lines of trenches, forming
a defensive belt two to three miles deep. Seven miles
back was a similar line, and yet another lay 27 miles
behind the first. In the weeks before the Germans
attacked it was possible to lay very thick minefields
with, in places, no fewer than 2400 anti-tank mines

per mile of front, with anti-personnel mines in addition. In guns, including antitank guns, the Russians
were stronger than the Germans, and in addition
they had their massed rocket launchers. Their aircraft also outnumbered the Germans. The number
of tanks and self-propelled guns made available,
including those of the reserves allocated to this
sector, was probably around 3500.

Unusually, the German attack began in the middle
of a hot afternoon, and this caught the Russians
partly off guard. After bombers had pounded the
Russians the XLVIII Panzer Corps pushed northward from the Kharkov Salient. Despite unexpected
rain during the night, this formation, supported by a
neighboring SS armored corps, succeeded in breaking through the first Russian defense line. But despite good air support (the Luftwaffe having gained
air superiority), the attack faltered during the second
day. Partly this was because of more, very heavy,
rainfall, which meant that what were usually small
streams required substantial bridgework by the
sappers. The thickly laid mines, well-directed Soviet
artillery fire, and the excellent morale of the Soviet
infantry were other important factors.

While the thrust from the south proceeded slower
than expected, Model's advance from the north

petered out quite early. It had begun on 5 July, at the more conventional hour of dawn, and had managed to break through the first Soviet line at the end of the day. But by the next day the Soviet command had managed to bring substantial reinforcement to this sector. German infantrymen took heavy casualties in a series of small engagements, and the armor, which included some Tigers and Ferdinands, began to run short of ammunition. The Russians continued to lay mines, even in areas which had been cleared by tank rollers, and losses from these were quite substantial. By this stage, hardly two days from the start, Model's forces were blocked, and Russian reinforcements were still arriving.

In the south of the Salient XLVIII and II SS Panzer Corps of the Fourth Panzer Army continued to struggle forward. In this sector the operations of the German dive-bombers were increasingly hampered by Soviet fighters. Soviet reinforcements, including specialized antitank units, had moved up behind the second line of defenses, where some tanks were dug in to serve as well-protected antitank guns. For a short period, when a panzer corps from the Kempf Group moved up to support the other panzer corps, it seemed that a break to Oboyan might be achieved, but strong Soviet artillery, with flank

attacks against the Fourth Panzer Army, then absorbed the remaining German momentum.

Part of the German failure may certainly be ascribed to bad luck, and notably the untimely rainfall. But much was due to the thorough Russian preparation and to the skill with which reserves were rushed to hard-pressed sectors. As was the usual Soviet practice, a reserve front (named Steppe Front) had been assembled well in the rear, and this proved a great asset. In addition to all this the German armor was not well handled. The employment of new and only partially tested Panther and Tiger tanks proved the wisdom of the pessimists. Their vaunted 88mm guns, and those of the Ferdinands, had not been supported by adequate ammunition stocks. The Ferdinand lacked machine guns to defend itself against short-range infantry attacks, and the Panther had a small design fault which resulted in spontaneous outbreaks of fire. And even the 88mm ammunition which was available was wasted, because the heavy tanks were put at the head of the medium tanks; this meant that they tended to engage at close quarters, where a 75mm gun was just as effective as an 88mm.

The great tank battle of Prokhorovka took place on 12 July. On the German side it was II SS Panzer

Above: Captured German Mark IV tanks are examined by Red Army men near Belgorod. The nearest tank carries additional armor to give protection against high-explosive antitank ammunition.

Corps which fought the main engagement, against the Soviet Fifth Guards Tank Army, commanded by the somewhat intellectual General Rotmistrov. A secondary engagement was between XLVIII Panzer Corps and the Soviet First Tank Army supported by the Sixth Guards Infantry Army. The battle, which lasted several days, began when Rotmistrov's tanks and self-propelled guns, about 850 in all, attacked the rather weaker SS Panzer Corps. The terrain was broken and partially wooded, which robbed the German 88mm guns of their theoretical advantage, since engagements tended to be at short range. Many Soviet tanks were lost to German aircraft. One Soviet formation, II Guards Tank Corps, had the distinction of engaging in what was the first battle fought by a large tank force against aircraft alone. The Germans used dive-bombers, some of

which carried large antitank cannons. This engagement was won by the Luftwaffe, which destroyed about 50 Soviet tanks. In these days both sides lost hundreds of tanks, but the battle never reached a final result, for in the middle of it Hitler decided to withdraw the SS panzers, along with other troops. These units were to be immediately transferred to Italy, where Anglo-American landings had just taken place. This decision was resisted by von Manstein, who considered that the German armor was poised on the edge of victory. Whether he was right or not (and he was probably wrong, given the availability of Soviet reserves) the Soviet armor was left in possession of the field and could claim the victory. The first phase of the Battle of Kursk was over. It was the turn of the Red Army to begin its own offensives.

Right: A German assault gun closes in on a Russian position during Operation 'Zitadelle.'
Below: A Soviet tank crew examine a knocked-out Tiger tank. The dusty conditions prevailing on the Kursk battlefield helped the Russians close in to defeat even the heaviest German tanks.
Opposite: A Soviet veteran of the Kursk battle.

These offensives, which lasted for the rest of the year, were made all along the front, although most weight was directed toward the center and south. The first move was an attack on the Orel salient, taking advantage of the German weakness after the Kursk battle. Orel was captured from the Germans on 5 August. However, Model was able to evacuate his troops successfully; although they tried hard, the Red commanders were not yet able to achieve the massive encirclements which the Germans had managed in the early part of the war. In the south, Vatutin was applying very strong pressure against tired and depleted German formations. He slipped his guards tank armies into a gap which had developed between the Fourth Panzer Army and the Kempf Group. Hitler's order to hold Kharkov deprived von Manstein of troops which could have been used to fill this gap. Eventually he defied Hitler, and abandoned Kharkov for the last time. But by then it was too late to prevent Tolbukhin breaking through to Taganrog, on the Sea of Azov. Although the German corps there was able to break out of encirclement, further tactical withdrawals were forced upon the German command. Hitler reluctantly agreed to pull his forces from their bridgehead in the north Caucasus, and to allow von Kluge to take his southern sector back to the line of the Desna River. But the Führer still rejected any idea of abandoning the Donets Basin, which was beginning to supply Germany with iron ore. But fresh Soviet breakthroughs forced yet more withdrawals on the Germans, who were repeatedly imperiled by flanking movements and incipient encirclements. In mid-September the Voronezh Front was driving toward the Dniepr, threatening the German rear. Von Manstein thereupon forcefully persuaded Hitler to permit a withdrawal to the western bank of that river. Hotly pursued by the leading Soviet units, German formations then scurried back to the Dniepr. The Red Army established a few small and unpromising bridgeheads on the western bank and also mounted a big airborne operation with the same object. Perhaps because this was the first large-scale Soviet parachute drop (it involved about 7000 men), it was badly bungled. Because it was badly bungled,

Above: One of the new Panther tanks knocked out at Kursk. Although Hitler delayed the start of the battle to allow more of these weapons to be produced, minor design faults in the tank limited their effectiveness.
Right: Covered by mortar fire, Soviet infantry advance during the Kursk battle.

Left: General Rotmistrov (center), the Soviet Union's most perceptive tank specialist, who commanded the Fifth Guards Tank Army in the Kursk battle.
Below: Shturmoviks dive to the attack during the Kursk fighting.

A heavy machine gun
supports a Soviet
infantry company on
the edge of the Kursk
Salient in June 1943.

Above: German infantry check that a Soviet T-34 has indeed been abandoned before it is towed away to prevent the Soviets recovering it.

Below: The remains of a Panther tank near Prokhorovka, the furthest penetration of the southern German pincer at Kursk.

it became the last as well as the first Soviet attempt at this kind of operation. Dropped in the dark, which was bad enough, the parachutists also had the misfortune to land among a German panzer corps.

Nevertheless, eventually the Dniepr was forced. Moreover, Vatutin succeeded in capturing Kiev in early November, and then continued to Zhitomir. Earlier the Russians captured Zaporozhe, and could thereupon seal off access to the Crimea. Clearly, by the end of the year the Germans were on the run, even though their retreat was orderly and not accompanied by massive casualties. Hitler still hoped that a remnant of his Sixth Army, which had remained at Nikopol, would provide a bridgehead

for a new 1944 offensive. But it was now clear to most observers that the Soviet forces had been growing stronger, and the German weaker, for so long that the gap between them had become so wide as to put a German recovery out of the question.

One of the consequences of the 1943 retreat was that the district of Lokot, near Orel, was overrun by the Russians, bringing to an end a unique German experiment. This had been a self-governing territory headed by a Russian engineer who cooperated with the Germans. In return for this cooperation, the German civil administration had been withdrawn from this district. Elsewhere in the occupied territories similar fruitful attempts at cooperation did not occur, although an exception to the general policy of subjugation and exploitation was the scheme set up by the German Ministry of Eastern Affairs, which enabled young Russians to go to Germany on a kind of apprenticeship basis, where they were treated not as slave workers, but like German young men in the same occupations.

At this time the German army contained about one million former Soviet citizens. Most were prisoners of war, but many were deserters from the Red Army, and there were even Russians from the pre-war waves of emigration. These were all known as 'Hiwis', this being an abbreviation for the German word for volunteers. They were used strictly as auxiliaries; one of their main functions being the driving and care of the army transport horses. In 1942 the idea of using armed anti-Bolshevik forces had begun to attract attention in OKW. Already certain non-Russian nationalities of the Soviet Union were offering their services. Prominent among

these were the two divisions of Cossacks, commanded by a German general, who fought with the eventual aim of regaining their homelands for themselves. However, in the summer of 1942 the concept of forming units that were not inspired by nationalism, but by anti-Bolshevism, was mooted. The obvious candidate to head such an undertaking was General Vlasov, an intelligent and popular Soviet general whose Second Army had been encircled and captured at Volkhov. From the Soviet point of view, Vlasov had impeccable social origins, being the son of a peasant and with a revolutionary past. Before the war he had been military advisor to Chiang Kai-shek, and during the war he had been much praised, as well as decorated with the Order of the Red Banner. His defection to the German cause was therefore a severe blow to the Soviet government. In 1943, encouraged by the German General Staff, he published an appeal to the Russian people which was distributed to the prisoners of war, the *Hiwis*, and throughout the occupied territories. There was an apparent rise in the Red Army desertion rate, and thousands of Russians expressed interest in taking up arms against the Bolsheviks. Naturally enough, the best response came from the underfed inhabitants of prisoner of war camps, where the proposed army seemed to offer release from a fate worse than death. However, neither Hitler nor his minister for Eastern Affairs, Rosenberg, favored this idea. Among other things, it implied that racially inferior Russians would fight side by side with the Wehrmacht. So at the end of 1943 the project was abandoned, and for a time Vlasov returned to the status of prisoner of war. But the following year, with the Germans plainly

facing defeat, the idea was revived by Himmler, among others. Changing from the patronage of the High Command to that of the SS was unfortunate for Vlasov, but he had little choice in the matter. He did make some gains, among them being the removal of the Eastern Badge which Russian workers in Germany had been forced to wear and which invited degrading treatment. And then, with the blessings of the German Foreign Ministry, the Committee for the Liberation of Russia, headed by Vlasov, was established. This had its own army, the Russian Liberation Army (ROA). However, German fears and Himmler's deviousness resulted in the formation of only three divisions under Vlasov, and only a single battalion ever seems to have been formally committed against the Red Army. This occurred in Silesia in 1945 and the battle was noteworthy for the large number of Red troops who deserted to the other side; at that stage of the war, this was quite surprising, and suggests what might have been achieved if Vlasov's army had been organized much earlier, and had reached the strength of one million which had been proposed. After the war, members of the ROA were rounded up by the British and Americans, the Western allies' officers showing considerably less enthusiasm for this task than the ministers and civil servants in London and Washington. The ROA men, together with other unwilling Russians, were then returned to the USSR, where an unpleasant fate awaited them. Among them was Vlasov, for whom a public execution was arranged in Moscow's Red Square in 1946. It was execution by hanging, for which purpose a meat hook is said to have been used.

Below: In the occupied zones wrecked Soviet factories were restored to production by German companies. Here Russians remove the Krupp signboard from a Kramatorsk engineering works, during the recapture of the Donets basin in 1943.

1943, a year in which both sides had their successes and failures, had clearly ended with the Germans in serious difficulty. The Battle of the Kursk Salient had been the first occasion when a German offensive had been halted virtually on its own start line, and from then onward the Wehrmacht had been conducting a fairly orderly though nevertheless extemporary withdrawal, considerably hindered by Hitler's insistence on rigidity. On the basis of the 1943 counteroffensives, the Soviet command envisaged a series of really big advances in 1944. These, though classified as the spring, summer and winter offensives, were an almost continuous succession of attacks. First on one front then on another, the Germans were pushed back, forcing tactical withdrawals on other fronts. The Red Army was now fast-moving in its motorized transport, but this advantage was not exploited by making deep rapid

thrusts, like the Germans had done in 1941 and 1942, but was used to shift the weight of attack rapidly from one sector to another, from one front to another. When German resistance stiffened in one locality, the Red Army relaxed its pressure and attacked somewhere else. In so doing it saved time and casualties, although frontal attacks were still the main method. The Germans suffered increasingly not only from material and manpower weaknesses, but from poor lateral communications. North-south railways were sparse, and the Red Army made a point of advancing to cut railway lines and capture junctions, with the result that it was usually impossible for one German Army Group to send reinforcements to another.

The Soviet propagandists called 1944 the 'Year of the Ten Victories': Leningrad was relieved, Sevastopol and the Crimea were recaptured, the Finns were pushed back and then left the war, the Vistula was reached in Poland, the Germans were either expelled or encircled in the Baltic states, the Red Army entered Hungary and Yugoslavia, Rumania surrendered, Bulgaria (which had initially declared war against Britain but not against the Soviet Union) was invaded.

Apart from these ten great achievements, lesser military successes were reported almost daily. Big victories, and especially the recapture of cities, were celebrated in Orders of the Day and gun salutes in Moscow. Several Soviet generals exhibited almost childish satisfactions and envy in the matter of these salutes; on neighboring sectors of a front, the question of which unit should liberate the next city was decided with a great deal of acrimony and jealousy. Possibly this competitive spirit was welcome to Stalin, but the haste with which commanders tried to capture big, salute-worthy, objectives sometimes led to casualties which in other armies would have been regarded as excessive.

In early 1944 several secondary offensives laid the foundation for the main attacks. In January, taking advantage of the ice on rivers and lakes, Novgorod

Previous page: **German infantry and armor on the march near Kovel in early 1944.**

Above: **General Chuikov (center) whose 8th Guards Army fought with the First Belorussian Front in 1944.**

Right: **General Model (center) with his staff officers.**

and Novosokolniki, and then Luga, were recaptured, forcing Army Group North to undertake a general retirement which finally relieved besieged Leningrad. In the center, in February, Vatutin captured Rovno and Lutsk and thereby threatened Galicia. Further south, Konev managed to encircle eight German divisions south of Kiev, while Malinovski broke through to capture Krivoi Rog in the Donets Basin.

In March, under the supervision of Zhukov and Vasilievsky, the Ukrainian fronts began the spring offensive. German resistance was shattered and the Wehrmacht's retreat was hurried and uncoordinated; the advancing Russians even managed to capture a German base at Uman containing 500 precious tanks. Konev's 2nd Ukrainian Front continued westward and at the end of the month had reached the River Prut. Meanwhile Zhukov, who for this

operation had taken over the 1st Ukrainian Front from Vatutin, crossed the Dniestr to occupy Chernovtsy, a railway junction, severing the link between the German forces in Poland and those in the south. Further south, Malinovsky captured Kherson and Nikolayev and the Rumanians abandoned Odessa without fighting. By the end of April Malinovsky had reached the Dniestr and was in contact with Konev's front.

This left strong German forces blocked in the Crimea. Tolbukhin's 4th Ukrainian Front was entrusted with the capture of the Crimea, and its staff conceived an enterprising plan whose main feature would be a crossing of the Sivash lagoons across the ice at the same time as a conventional attack was launched over the Perekop Isthmus. Unfortunately, the Sivash showed no signs of freezing so, recalling the Civil War capture of the Crimea, Tolbukhin sent his infantry into the lagoon without benefit of ice. Sure enough, they found enough shallow stretches to make wading practical. Rafts and pontoons were also found, and the crossing was made. This took place just as the Red forces had breached the first line of defenses at Perekop and assured the success of the operation. The Rumanians

Top: A German 75mm antitank gun said to have knocked out three tanks in three minutes.
Above: Yak-9 fighters photographed near Sevastopol in 1944. The Yak-9 was armed with a 20mm cannon and two heavy machine guns.
Left: Himmler and Hitler lead a group of Axis dignitaries at Hitler's headquarters after the assassination attempt against the Führer.

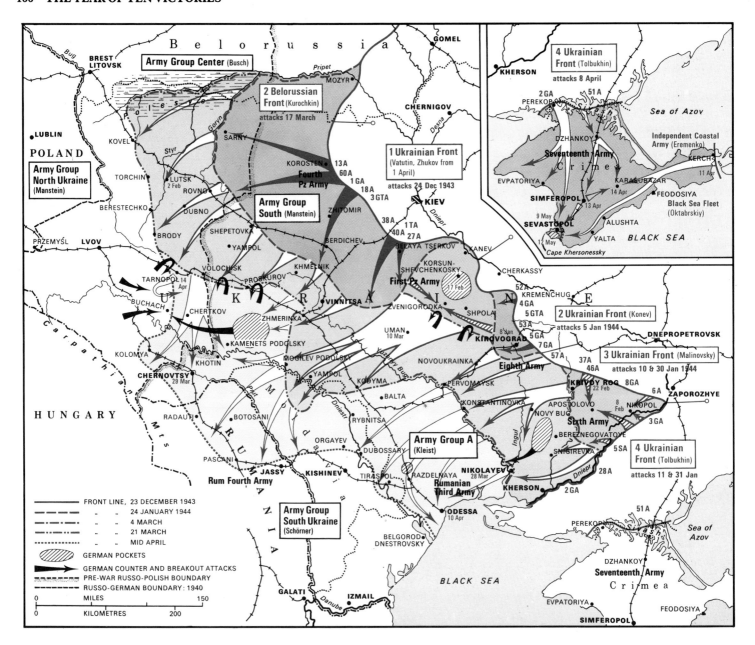

Above: The Soviet winter offensive, 1943-44.

and Germans retreated south to Sevastopol, which fell into Russian hands in early May; the Red Army thereby took complete control of the Crimea. By the end of the spring offensives, therefore, apart from a German salient which remained around the Pinsk Marshes, the pre-war Soviet boundaries had been reached by the Red Army.

The summer offensive coincided with the Anglo-American landings in Normandy. The first drive was on the Finnish front, the Karelian Isthmus being taken and then the city of Viborg.

One withdrawal led to another, although finally the Finns were able to hold a new line, and despite visits to Helsinki by the German foreign minister, Ribbentrop, and by Keitel, the Finnish government decided to negotiate a peace with Moscow. Partly because the war was not yet won, partly because the obstinacy and persistence of the Finns had been experienced in 1939–40, the peace terms were relatively light: Petsamo went to Russia, which also was to lease a base on the Porkkala Peninsula, and substantial reparations were to be paid. This ended what might be called the second Russo-Finnish War. It had been a war with peculiarities, and was virtually

a sideshow to the main campaigns. The Finns had wanted merely to win back their 1939 frontiers, whereas their German helpers had wanted considerably more, notably the assistance of the Finns in the Leningrad area and an advance eastward to capture Murmansk, preceded by a cutting of the Murmansk Railway. German troops, including a mountain corps for operations against Murmansk, had taken up positions in Finland well before the war began, but they had little success. Around Murmansk the Russians had command of the sea and, usually, of the air, while their troops made good use of the rugged terrain. The Germans never penetrated more than about 15 miles. Further south, the joint German-Finnish drive to cut the railway at Kandalaksha also failed. The SS troops which were part of the German contribution showed themselves as inferior fighters in the forests of this region, and the German command resented Finnish comments on this inferiority. Animosity grew between the Finnish and the German commander, von Falkenhorst, when the former suspected that Finnish troops were being entrusted with the most difficult operations. By the end of 1941, both here and in

Karelia (where a little more success rewarded the advance) the Finns had begun their policy of sullen cooperation at times and places of their own, not German, choosing. The Murmansk Railway was in fact cut near Lake Lodoga, but this was of little use because the Russians laid a connecting line between Belomorsk and the parallel Archangel Railway, so Anglo-American supplies continued to move from Murmansk.

The final phase of the Finnish war came in 1944, after peace had been made with Russia; Finnish troops turned against their redundant allies, the Germans, and drove them out of the country. The withdrawal of Finland from the war released Soviet

Above: Sappers from the 2nd Belorussian Front bridge the River Narew.
Left: General Lelyushenko, commander of the 3rd Tank Army, during the advance to Lvov.

Below: Partisans from the Odessa catacombs emerge after the recapture of the city.

КОЛХОЗНИКА
ОНЕВА
силия Викторовича

forces for use against Army Group North. In October Riga had to be abandoned and Army Group North withdrew into Courland, the northern part of Latvia. Here it remained, being by-passed by the main Russian offensives. Supplied by sea it was still fighting at the time of the German surrender.

The second major summer offensive opened at the end of June, and was directed against the German 'hedgehogs' and armies in the triangle Minsk–Vitebsk–Zhlobin. This was quickly accomplished, partly because Hitler's preference for 'hedgehog' defense meant that German forces lost their mobility. As early as 3 July Minsk was captured. The subsequent grasp of Vilna and Grodno, and a bridgehead across the Nieman, meant that for the first time German home territory, in East Prussia, was threatened. Further north, Army Group North came under attack by the fronts of Eremenko and Masslenikov. The weak German defense lines, unsupported by any significant reserves, were broken through, with Ostrov, Pskov and Narva soon being taken.

In the south, Tolbukhin advanced into Rumania in August and after the capture of Jassy King Michael was persuaded to dismiss the Antonescu government which, despite its quarrels with Hitler, was still regarded as the latter's ally. Negotiations with the Allies did not bring an immediate peace, but by the end of August the Red Army was in control of the capital, Bucharest, having destroyed the German Sixth Army in an encirclement action near Kishinev. Hitler's prized Ploesti oilfields were occupied at the same time.

The rapidity of the Soviet advances came as a surprise to both Russia's enemies and friends. One factor was the practice of not halting an advance to destroy pockets of encircled German formations. Sometimes the Germans were able to extricate a proportion of their encircled men by breakouts, but usually such pockets were allowed to languish until such time as Soviet infantry had time to deal with them. Normally this was not long, because there was no shortage of troops. On the German side the situation was completely different. There was not only a numerical deficiency, but newly arriving troops tended to be of inferior quality. Partly this was because they were from older age-groups, partly because they were only skimpily trained. The old training system, in which the 'Replacement Army' was maintained solely as a training formation, had long ago been changed on Hitler's instructions, and since then the situation had further deteriorated. Specialized arms suffered particularly from this, as they depended on superbly trained men to compensate for their deficiency in numbers. This was evident among sappers, gunners, and tank crews, but was especially noticeable in the Luftwaffe where, because of fuel shortage, training flights were curtailed and sometimes cancelled altogether. Shortage of aviation fuel also meant that the Luftwaffe was

Above: Soviet soldiers capture a Rumanian castle during the fighting for the town of Jassy in the late summer of 1944. *Opposite:* Ivan Kozhedub, the top-scoring Soviet fighter pilot of the war, seen in the cockpit of an aircraft said to have been donated by a collective farm and inscribed accordingly.

Right: General
Rokossovsky at his
headquarters in 1944.
Below: German Tiger
tanks ford a river near
Tarnopol in April
1944. Tiger tanks were
normally deployed in
independent heavy
tank battalions rather
than as part of the
armored divisions.
Bottom: Konev,
commander of the 1st
Ukraine Front, in
1944.

forced to limit its reconnaissance flights, denying the
army command of valuable intelligence. Speculative
sorties were also impracticable, and so, usually, was
the provision of permanent air cover. Added to all
this was the necessity of deploying the higher-
quality machines and crews to meet the Anglo-
American air offensive. During 1944, therefore,
Soviet air superiority over the Eastern Front
became overwhelming, which was yet another
reason for the degeneration of the Wehrmacht into an
uncoordinated army which seemed sometimes on the
verge of collapse. Not only were its formations
harried from the air, but Soviet attacks were directed
at putting out of action the few good roads, thereby
hampering the swift movement of troops from one
sector to another.

Meanwhile von Manstein, whose retreats had
irritated Hitler, had been replaced by Model, in

whom the Führer placed great faith. Model commanded both Army Group South and Army Group Center, which collectively were known as Army Group North Ukraine. Despite some success in creating a stronger defensive line, Model did not improve on von Manstein's performance. He had lost Minsk, and soon Rokossovsky took Brest Litovsk and advanced to the Vistula, where he made three crossings at the end of July. On the last day of July the Germans retreated into Warsaw.

These events persuaded the Polish Home Army, the Polish resistance movement, to begin a long-planned uprising in Warsaw. Obviously this was both the most propitious and useful moment. Propitious because the rising would make still more difficult the German predicament, propitious because it would probably result in Russian troops entering a city that was already in Polish hands. But when the Red forces reached the River Vistula, on the opposite bank of which lay Warsaw, they halted and did not advance for several weeks. This enabled the Germans to suppress the rising. The Polish Home Army carried on the bloody struggle for some weeks, street by street, and when it eventually surrendered most of its members were dead. Subsequently the USSR was blamed for this tragic result. Certainly, Moscow radio broadcasts to Poland had encouraged a rising; certainly, the Red Army unaccountably came to a halt virtually at the gates of Warsaw; certainly, Stalin refused landing facilities to aircraft which the Anglo-Americans were proposing to send on supply-dropping missions to Warsaw. Certainly, too, Stalin had little love for the Polish Home Army, which he regarded as a tool of the London Polish government and therefore hostile to the Moscow-based Polish government which was being groomed

Below: Guns of the 2nd Belorussian Front in 1944. By that year the Red Army was able to provide massive artillery concentrations to support its advancing troops.

Below: Paulus signs the 'Free Germany' appeal to Germans to overthrow Hitler. Paulus also made radio broadcasts on behalf of the Russians.
Bottom: Göring (center) and other officers examine the wreckage left by the bomb attack on Hitler in July 1944.

to take power. On the other hand the Soviet explanation, that the advancing Red Army was in urgent need of rest and recuperation, and was indeed in no condition to embark on an immediate battle for Warsaw, has a ring of truth about it. The Soviet offensive had been very fast and had covered an enormous distance; there can be little doubt that it had somewhat outrun its supply services. Whatever the truth, the incident was a further contribution to the souring of Russo-Polish relations, never very warm in the best of circumstances. The discovery by the Germans in 1943 of a mass grave containing the bodies of Polish officers captured by the Red Army in 1939 and massacred at Katyn, presumably by the NKVD, was another deeply felt grievance.

In the Balkans, Bulgaria decided to declare war against Germany, but the use of its territory by the advancing Red Army would have occurred in any case. The Russians were therefore able to advance into Hungary and Yugoslavia on a broad front. In Yugoslavia, they allowed Tito to capture Belgrade before their own troops entered. They soon left Yugoslavia and concentrated on the drive into

Hungary. The Hungarian regent, Horthy, had earlier decided to break his alliance with Hitler, but was thereupon deposed by the Germans, who took control of the country. But this did nothing to halt the Russian advance over the Hungarian plains towards Budapest. However, despite recent heavy losses in Rumania, where 16 German divisions had been encircled and others destroyed, Budapest was to be strongly defended. By Christmas, although the Russians held most of Hungary, they had still not taken the Hungarian capital.

The supply of the German formations cut off in Courland was a final demonstration of the potentialities of naval superiority. Neither Hitler nor Stalin had a great understanding, or enthusiasm, for naval activities, and this is a partial explanation for the lack of enterprise shown by the naval forces on each side. Geography dictated that a Russo-German war would be primarily a land war, but the contribution made by naval forces could have been greater than it was. The naval war, such as it was, was fought

Left: Vitebsk is captured by the 1st Baltic Front. Because of heavy fighting and German demolition, most recaptured cities were in ruins.

Above: Troops of the 4th Ukraine Front plod over the Polish Carpathians in the winter of 1944-45.

in three major theaters, the Baltic, Black and Barents seas, with minor Red Navy units active also on certain inland rivers and lakes. The conditions of the three major theaters were so different that they are best dealt with separately.

In the Baltic the Red Navy had a clear-cut material preponderance. The German navy was small in any case, and the bulk of its strength was directed against Britain. In the Baltic it maintained only small vessels, preponderantly minelayers and minesweepers, motor torpedo boats and a few submarines. The Red Baltic Squadron, by contrast, possessed two old but heavily gunned battleships, two heavy cruisers, 14 modern destroyers and no fewer than 65 submarines. It was based on Tallinn (Reval), Riga, Libau and Kronstadt. In summer 1941 both sides concentrated on laying minefields; in fact the Germans were laying mines even before the war started, with the result that when Soviet minelaying began, a covering destroyer was sunk and a heavy cruiser badly damaged. As the Germans advanced

along the Baltic coast, the Russian bases fell and those ships which had not been excessively damaged were transferred to the main base at Kronstadt. The Soviet submarines had few successes, and several were lost, usually to mines. The Navy suffered heavy losses in its partially successful and quite heroic evacuation of troops from Reval. Most of these losses were caused by air attack, and some by mines.

In the Gulf of Riga there was a mystifying engagement in July, when Soviet destroyers on a minelaying mission encountered a German supply convoy escorted by a handful of lightly armed and slow minesweepers. The Russians opened fire, but steadfastly refused to press their attack, and eventually retired. This is perhaps the clearest example of the lack of boldness which characterized so many Red naval operations. Possibly the reluctance to act without written orders contributed to this; on this occasion the Russian commander probably had detailed orders for his minelaying mission, but no orders to cover unexpected events.

Light and heavy machine guns in the front line east of Warsaw as Red Army officers confer. *Inset:* The Belorussian and Ukrainian campaigns of the summer of 1944.

Map labels:

TUKUMS · 31 July · RIGA · Latvia · Army Group North (Lindemann*)
LIEPAJA · AUCE · JELGAVA · REZEKNE · 10 GA · TOROPETS
BALTIC SEA · JEKABPILS · Dvina · Sixteenth Army · 3 SA · 1 Baltic Front (Bagramyan)
MEMEL · SIAULIAI · DAUGAVPILS (DVINSK) · 22 A · NEVEL · 4 SA
PANEVEZYS · 6 GA · 43 A
Lithuania · DISNA · GLUBOKOYE · POLOTSK · 39 A · 3 Belorussian Front (Chernyakhovsky)
TILSIT · Niemen · VITEBSK · 5 GTA · 5 A
KÖNIGSBERG · KAUNAS · 13 July · LEPEL · Third Pz Army · 11 GA · SMOLENSK
INSTERBURG · VILNYUS · ORSHA · 31 A
EAST PRUSSIA · BORISOV · 33 A · 49 A · ROSLAVL
SUWALKI · Fourth Army · MOGILEV · 50 A
ALLENSTEIN · GRODNO · Army Group Center (Busch†) · MINSK · 1 July · 2 Belorussian Front (Zakharov)
JOHANNISBURG · NOVOGRUDOK · Berezina · Druf
Belorussia · 3 A · STARODUB
Narew · BIAŁYSTOK · Ninth Army · BOBRUYSK · ROGACHEV
SLONIM · BARON · VICHI · SLUTSK · 48 A
BEREZA · BYTEN · LYUBAN · GOMEL
WOŁOMIN · Second Army · Pripet · 65 A
WARSAW · 28 July · KOBRIN · PINSK · Pripet · 28 A
BREST-LITOVSK · Marshes · CHERNIGOV
POLAND · 61 A
MAGNUSZEW · PUŁAWY · 70 A / 47 A / 8 GA · 1 Belorussian Front (Rokossovsky)
LUBLIN · KOVEL · SARNY · KOROSTEN · Dniepr
CHEŁM · 2 TA
Fourth Pz Army · 69 A · VLADIMIR VOLYNSKIY · 3 GA · LUTSK · 1 GTA · Ukraine
SANDOMIERZ · Vistula · MIELEC · KHOLOYUV · 13 A · DUBNO · ZHITOMIR · KIEV
TARNOW · First Pz Army · LVOV · 1 Ukrainian Front (Konev)
JASLO · PRZEMYSL · 27 July · First Hun Army · 60 A · TARNOPOL · 3 GTA / 4 TA
Army Group N Ukraine (Model) · SAMBOR · 38 A · 4 Ukrainian Front (Petrov) (from 5 Aug 1944)
Slovakia · STRY · 1 GA
STANISLAV · Dniestr
NADVORNAYA · 18 A
UZHGOROD · KOLOMIN
NYIREGYHAZA · KHOTIN · CHERNOVTSY
HUNGARY · (From Rumania) · RUMANIA

FRONT LINES : 1944

	BELORUSSIA	UKRAINE
	22 JUNE	13 JULY
	4 JULY	18 JULY
	28 JULY	28 JULY
	29 AUGUST	29 AUGUST

→ GERMAN COUNTERATTACKS
GERMAN POCKETS
PRE-WAR RUSSO-POLISH BOUNDARY
RUSSO-GERMAN BOUNDARY : 1940

0 — MILES — 150
0 — KILOMETERS — 250

*Friessner later, then Schörner † Model later, then Reinhardt

Opposite: Soviet antitank gunners in action in the approaches to Poznan. *Below:* A Focke-Wulf 190 fighter, one of the Luftwaffe's best designs, in flight over Rumania during the fighting in 1944.

Another costly evacuation was aimed at rescuing the Russian garrison from the Finland base of Hango, which cost the Baltic Squadron three destroyers. On the whole, throughout the war, the Red Navy was regarded simply as an adjunct to the Red Army even though, unlike the Air Force, it had its own independent existence and administration. This was emphasized when the Germans closed on Leningrad, and their tanks encountered long-range heavy shells from Soviet battleships and cruisers. German dive-bombers thereupon attacked, and the battleship *Marat* was sunk. But since the water was shallow in the Leningrad commercial port, where she was stationed, she rested on the bottom and her guns remained active until the Germans left the vicinity in 1944.

But this was the only activity of the Soviet heavy ships. They never moved far, not even in 1944 and 1945 when the Germans introduced some heavy ships in the Baltic, with which they damagingly bombarded the advancing Soviet armies. Fear of losses seems to have been the main cause of this reluctance; such fears were perhaps justified, given the danger from mines and submarines. Possibly there was a shortage of crews, for in the siege of Leningrad most of the sailors had been drafted ashore to take part in the land fighting, but leaving the ships in harbor was a travesty of the proper use of naval power.

When the Soviet offensive began, there were occasional amphibious operations designed to disturb the enemy's rear. Those undertaken against coastal objectives were usually unsuccessful at first, but lessons were learned from mistakes and by 1945 these enterprises were occasionally blessed with success, although they had little effect on the outcome of the war. In the final year, the Red Navy's air squadrons began to enjoy greater success. By that time the Luftwaffe, whose relationship with the German navy had never been good, was unable as well as unwilling to provide fighter escorts, while the Russians made good use of the American-supplied Boston torpedo and bombing aircraft. Soviet air attacks were not pushed home with any great dash, reliance being placed on a close succession of attacks in the expectation that the German naval escorts would either become tired, or run out of ammunition.

The Soviet submarine force was relatively unsuccessful. It lost many boats on minefields and its crews were not well-trained, so that opportunities which did present themselves were usually missed. However, the presence of so many submarines induced the Finns and Germans to lay a steel net across the mouth of the Gulf of Finland and for two years, until Finland left the war, this kept Soviet submarines out of the Baltic. Earlier, in 1942, Soviet submarines had occasionally attacked the iron ore traffic passing from Sweden to Germany, and sank several vessels flying the Swedish flag.

In 1944 it was the turn of the Germans to evacuate their troops from Baltic shores. Typically, as the

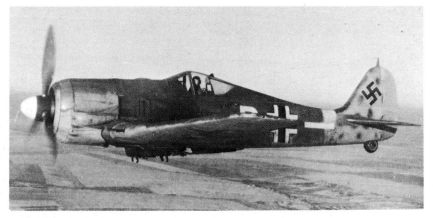

Above: Red Navy destroyers in the Barents Sea in 1942. The Red Navy made comparatively little contribution to the protection of the Allied supply convoys sailing to the northern ports. *Right:* A K-type submarine of the Northern Fleet.

Red Army advanced, pockets of German troops would be cut off and rescued by German small craft. The Germans brought two pocket battleships and a cruiser into the Baltic to provide support for these evacuations and to provide gunfire support for the army. The absence of any attack by Russian surface ships on these vessels was less surprising than the absence of any submarine activity. It seems probable that by the time the submarine commanders received their orders, the German ships had changed their positions. Only naval aircraft attacked the German ships, with little success. Absence of Soviet naval intervention enabled the Germans to supply their 600,000 strong army in Courland without trouble and with almost no loss. Even more spectacular, in the closing months of the war, was the evacuation of more than two million German soldiers and refugees encircled by the Russian advance on the Pomeranian coast near Danzig; some thousands of these fugitives were lost when their transports were sunk or damaged by Soviet air attack, but in the main the evacuation was successful; only intervention by Soviet surface ships could have prevented it, and these ships were kept in harbor at Kronstadt and Leningrad.

In the Black Sea the Red Navy showed more enterprise than in the Baltic, especially in the early part of the war. On this sea, too, Russia had naval superiority. The squadron included a battleship, *Parizhskaya Kommuna*, which was old but had heavy (12-inch) guns. There were also five cruisers, 13 destroyers, and 47 submarines. Rumania possessed just four destroyers and a submarine. The Germans were able to transport six 250-ton submarines to the Black Sea down the Danube, as well as motor torpedo boats and minesweepers.

As early as 26 June 1941 two modern Soviet

destroyers closed the Rumanian port of Constanta and carried out a quite effective bombardment; but the operation ended when they ran onto a minefield and the destroyer *Moskva* was sunk. Perhaps the peak of the Red Navy's performance in this sea were the Odessa operations of 1941. This city held out under siege from August to October, somewhat disrupting the invasion schedule. Throughout this period it was supplied by the Red Navy, which also removed its wounded. The Navy also carried out a highly successful landing behind the besieging Rumanians' lines, causing them to withdraw in some disorder. Then, in October, the evacuation by sea began. This was carried out so competently that the Rumanians were unaware, in the final days, how few defenders were left. In the first half of October about 86,000 soldiers, 150,000 civilians, and considerable material was taken away. When the Rumanians entered the city there were only 6000 Russian soldiers left. Losses, all from air attack, probably did not exceed three small transports.

Most of the troops taken from Odessa were delivered to Sevastopol, considerably strengthening the defenses there. This fortified naval base held out until 1942, again considerably disrupting the German plans. Throughout the siege the Red Navy was active, undertaking several amphibious landings on the Crimean coast to relieve the pressure on Sevastopol. The most notable such landing was at Feodosiya in December 1941, in which two cruisers and seven destroyers took part and 40,000 troops were landed. Here they threatened to expand their bridgehead throughout the Crimea and strong forces had to be diverted to contain them and, in January, force them to re-embark, which they did in good order.

In 1942 the Soviet ships frequently made shore bombardments, and there were few qualms about

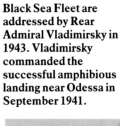

Below: Sailors of the Black Sea Fleet are addressed by Rear Admiral Vladimirsky in 1943. Vladimirsky commanded the successful amphibious landing near Odessa in September 1941.

risking *Parizhskaya Kommuna* in these activities; this vessel even carried wounded from Sevastopol, her home base. But in May, for some reason, the navy failed to make any real rescue attempt on behalf of 150,000 Red troops who were cut off in the Kerch Peninsula and duly taken prisoner. Sevastopol fell at the end of June. Because Stalin had forbidden evacuation it was not possible to repeat the triumph of Odessa, and German air activity would have made such an enterprise quite costly. The last major warship to leave Sevastopol was the large destroyer *Tashkent*, which carried a thousand men in and brought out more than double that number of wounded and civilians. She was so damaged by air attack that when she struggled into the port of Novorossiisk she subsided on to the bottom.

In 1942 there was a good deal of naval activity around the Kerch Strait, largely by motor torpedo boats, occasionally supported by heavier vessels. The main target was the German traffic across that Strait, supplying the forces in the Caucasus. Amphibious raids were also undertaken from time to time. When the Germans captured Novorossiisk the Red ships had to use commercial ports further down the coast, and their reduced role henceforth was possibly because of this disadvantage; after so much action they would have been in need of maintenance and repair, which were now hard to provide. Also, after three destroyers attempting to molest German supply convoys off the Crimea had been destroyed by dive bombers in 1943, Stalin appears to have disapproved activities involving the larger warships.

The Germans used small vessels in their supply convoys, and very few of these were sunk. It was thanks to their sea route along the coast that the Crimea was able to hold out so long. The most frequent attacks came from the air, but such attacks

Above: Naval Commander in chief Kuznetsov (center) with Zhukov (left) at the Potsdam conference in 1945. *Left:* The destroyer *Opytnyi*, cut off in Leningrad, contributes its guns to the defense in 1942.

Above: A Red Navy vessel supports shore operations with short-range rockets in the 1944 Baltic operations.

were rarely pressed home when the ships carried antiaircraft guns. The sinkings were therefore considerably less than the number of attacks made. In 1943 there were about 300 air attacks on German convoys, but only three small steamers and eight lighters were sunk, together with a few small escorting ships.

The Black Sea submarines were active to some degree throughout the war. As in the Baltic, a large number of neutral ships were sunk, probably because inexperienced submarine commanders fired their torpedoes without troubling to ascertain the identity of their targets. Turkish ships were frequent victims, and there were tragic cases of ships carrying Jewish refugees being sunk. However, the sinkings made by Soviet submarines were infrequent, and very small in relation to the number of submarines available. About 20 submarines were lost in the Black Sea war.

German seaborne evacuations in 1944 were not unmolested, but were largely unaffected, by Soviet naval attack. The biggest evacuation was that of the Crimea, which could have been almost bloodless had Hitler not given one of his 'fight to the last man' instructions. But despite this order, 80,000 men were moved by sea to Constanta, without loss, despite the nine Russian submarines lying in wait between the Crimea and Rumania. It was only the last 30,000, taken off at the last moment with Hitler's agreement, who suffered. With no Luftwaffe cover, the convoys had to rely on their own resources for antiaircraft protection, and in due course many of them ran out of ammunition. A number of ships were sunk, and about 8000 men drowned. But this was a small proportion of the total evacuated and the Germans would have suffered a major disaster if the Soviet surface ships had boldly attacked them.

The Red Navy's operations in the Sea of Azov were independent, for the most part, of the Black Sea operations. Commander of the naval forces in the Azov Sea was Admiral Gorshkov, who was subsequently to inspire and supervise the creation of a modern, powerful and influential Soviet Fleet as head of the Soviet Navy under Khrushchev, Brezhnev and Andropov. In 1941 he was a Captain, First Rank (Commodore) and carried out the highly successful amphibious landing behind the Rumanian lines outside Odessa. This, and subsequent distinction, presumably led to his promotion to Rear Admiral in command of the Azov flotilla.

In many ways the Soviet Arctic Squadron, though much smaller than those in the Black Sea, Baltic and Far East, played a more active and successful role in the war. Its main base was at Polyarnyi (Murmansk), which was ice-free throughout the year. It consisted of only eight destroyers, three torpedo boats, 21 submarines, 20 motor torpedo boats and many smaller craft, although during the war it was reinforced and even came to include a battleship. When the war started the Germans, with an imperfect appreciation of the advantages of sea power in this region, launched their thrust on Murmansk overland, employing General Dietl's mountain corps, which had achieved such good results against the French and British in Norway. Thanks to the ability of the Russians to land and supply troops in the Rybachii Peninsula, they were able to hold the German drive there, and from that strategically advantageous position make further German advance impossible. So although it was hardly 30 miles from the frontiers of Finland and Norway to Murmansk, the Germans never succeeded in penetrating more than halfway. Although German bombing attacks were made, the low priority which this theater enjoyed meant that insufficient aircraft were available to prevent the Russian ships continuing to support the Red troops by bombardments, landings, and supply operations. Dietl soon discovered, like commanders of German formations elsewhere on the Eastern Front, that the maps supplied to him showed roads which in reality did not exist. This not only delayed his advance in the first crucial weeks but meant that throughout these operations, which continued until Finland left the war in 1944, German supplies had to be passed along the northern coast of Norway in convoys of small ships which were vulnerable to attacks by the Red Navy. A small German destroyer flotilla was sent into this theater in summer 1941 to protect these convoys, and also to attack Soviet shipping; it was later supplemented by small armed minesweepers. British ships were also active in these waters, especially when Anglo-American convoys to Russia were in the area. As early as September 1941 the British cruisers *Aurora* and *Nigeria* sank a large convoy escort, the *Bremse*, and almost caught the laden troop transports she was convoying. Both British and Soviet submarines patrolled the shipping routes, but in 1941 they had negligible success. It was two British submarines, *Tigris* and *Trident*, which from August to December operated from Polyarnyi, that made the only important sinkings. The Soviet submarines sank only a few small ships, but reported many considerable victories. This discrepancy, which continued throughout the war and was also evident in reports made by the Baltic and Black Sea squadrons, had several explanations. Commanders tended to overestimate the size of the ships they attacked, from lack of experience and haste. There was also a tendency, already widespread in Soviet industry, deliberately to exaggerate achievements. Soviet commanders listened for the detonation of their torpedoes, and such detonations were enough to claim a sinking, even though the torpedo might have detonated prematurely or hit a submerged rock. German U-Boats were active in the area right up to the end of the war. Although their main targets were the Anglo-American convoys, which were located by reconnaissance aircraft and then attacked by aircraft and submarines, they also attacked Soviet shipping in the White and Kara seas. In terms of tonnage sunk they were more successful than the Russian submarines but, like the latter, they suffered losses which were quite heavy in proportion to their numbers.

Soviet destroyers, like their German counterparts, laid minefields but did not seek action with enemy surface ships. Their contribution to the protection of convoys from Britain was negligible, although they escorted these convoys on the approaches to Murmansk and Archangel. Reinforcements arrived in 1942: three modern destroyers came via the Northern Sea Route, from the unemployed Far Eastern Squadron, while some submarines arrived from the Baltic via the Baltic-White Sea Canal. The Germans also transferred several of their largest warships to bases in northern Norway, where they could threaten the Anglo-American convoys. A pocket battleship, *Admiral Scheer*, made one excursion in the Kara Sea in 1942, but succeeded only in sinking a Russian icebreaker. Soviet attacks, both by aircraft and torpedo cutters, on German coastal convoys increased in 1942, but these were not pressed home and sinkings were few. But in that year the Soviet submarines sank several transports; their successes, however, were not commensurate either with their numbers or their days at sea. Nine submarines were lost, and to help replace losses six boats were sent from Vladivostok. These passed via the Aleutians, the Panama Canal, and Halifax, Nova Scotia. One of them was sunk by a Japanese submarine off the west coast of America, evidently having been mistaken for an American boat. In 1944 a similar misfortune overtook another submarine. This time it was one of four U-class boats handed over by the Royal Navy to Soviet crews for movement by the latter to Murmansk. It appears to have strayed from its prescribed path, and was sunk by a British bomber.

In the last three years of the war the Red Navy and its aircraft became somewhat more experienced, and the air strength was enhanced both in numbers and quality. The dropping of torpedoes on parachutes from aircraft was practiced here, as in the Black Sea, and was occasionally successful. The number of sinkings increased slowly, but never so much as really to threaten the Germans with catastrophe. When, in 1944, the German troops had to evacuate the far north, most went by sea.

Apart from submarines, the Red Navy in these waters received the elderly British battleship *Royal Sovereign* which, when taken over by Soviet crews, was renamed *Archangelsk*. She was the target of several unsuccessful U-Boat attacks, but appears to have played no role except, perhaps, as a deterrent. She spent the rest of the war tied up in Polyarnyi. An American four-funneled cruiser and some former US Navy four-funnel destroyers were also received. In part these acquisitions were despatched in place of the Soviet share of the Italian navy, which surrendered to the Allies in 1943.

Despite its achievements, especially in the second part of the war, the Red Navy in all three seas was considerably less successful than it should have been. On a number of occasions lack of boldness prevented it taking advantage of unanticipated opportunities. Part of its weakness was that until the late 1930s its development had been held back, so it consisted of ships laid down by the tsarist government and a few more-modern vessels started just before the war. Its newer cruisers and destroyers were designed with Italian assistance, Italians being chosen because the specifications, especially the speeds, of their ships, seemed so superior to those of the other naval powers. That Italian ships achieved their high trial speeds because their runs were made in calm waters, and in light condition for the event was not, apparently, realized by the Navy Ministry (or, more likely, was concealed from Stalin, who probably made the final decisions). Moreover, Italian ships were lightly built, and at least one Italian-design destroyer appears to have broken up in an Arctic storm.

Below: A Red Navy destroyer defends a convoy from air attack. *Bottom:* The *Gremyashchy*, a 'Guards' destroyer of the Northern Fleet. Units of all the Russian services which were held to have performed particularly distinguished service were given the 'Guards' designation.

When 1944 ended the Red Army had grown to about seven million men, including the Air Force. It had about 500 infantry divisions and its specialized arms had grown even faster; the infantryman was the factor in short supply now, not tanks and guns and aircraft as in 1941. It was supplemented, a little more than symbolically, by recently allocated Polish, Rumanian, Czech and Bulgarian divisions. Some Soviet prisoners of war, released by the Red Army, were re-conscripted by the latter. There were approaching 100 artillery divisions, and some of these were specialized rocket projector formations. The German Army and SS in the east was a little over two million strong, if field strength only be counted. Over one million more were fighting in Western Europe, where the long-expected Normandy landings had drawn fewer divisions from the Eastern Front than the Russians had hoped, although in mid-1944 less than half the German Army was engaged in the east. There were many transfers in both directions between east and west, and as Hitler became more nervous, and as his total of available troops diminished, the proportion of his forces which on any day was riding in trains from one front to another grew quite seriously. In France, in 1944, the Wehrmacht lost nearly 400,000 dead and missing, while in the same period (June–December) about double that number was lost fighting the Russians. It may be assumed that about 700,000 were wounded. So in those seven months the German Army must have permanently lost the services of about 1,500,000 men, a loss which could not be replaced. Over one hundred German divisions had been destroyed or damaged beyond repair in the fighting and the new divisions formed to replace them, and the surviving old divisions, were well under strength. Some divisions were mere skeletons, retained in being partly to deceive the Russians into thinking that the German Army was bigger than it really was. Hitler was well aware of this fact, but often he made decisions as though he was not, sending into action divisions which were hardly more than a few companies of dispirited men. He also assumed that the Soviet high command was playing the same tricks,

so when he was presented with evidence of the huge number of Red Army divisions on a particular front, he insisted that the number of men actually available must be much less; this was a useful argument when his generals tried to persuade him to accept a further withdrawal.

Qualitatively, despite the steady attrition of the most experienced German regulars, German soldiers and officers were still, on average, superior to their opponents. This is one reason, possibly the only substantial reason, why the Wehrmacht was able to fight so long and firmly in 1945. On the Vistula and East Prussian fronts, for example and according to Guderian, the Red Army had eleven times as many infantrymen, seven times as many tanks, and twenty times as many guns, yet met solid resistance. Despite the good German response as the Russians got closer to Berlin Hitler showed more and more distrust and animosity towards his army. The firing squad for officers alleged to have withdrawn without orders became a fairly frequent phenomenon. In August of 1944 it was decided that the next of kin of men deemed to have committed treason (that is, to have made an unwarranted withdrawal) should themselves be liable to punishment. The army was more heavily politicized. When Himmler was appointed commander of the Replacement Army, in which the new divisions were created, the term infantry division was replaced by the name *Volksgrenadier* division, a term more in keeping with Nazi ideology with its emphasis on that somewhat distorted concept, the *Volk*, or Germanic People. Also, Himmler's SS formed its own SS Army HQ, and ordinary army officers were compulsorily transferred to the SS to enable the formation of more SS corps HQ. Meanwhile political commissars (a term banned by Hitler, who was careful to call them National Socialist Party Representatives) had been attached to army units, where they were supposed to stiffen morale but in reality occupied themselves with spying on the soldiers and officers.

Making next-of-kin responsible for treasonous crimes, appointing commissars, creating and enhancing the SS formations, were all reminiscent of Soviet practice; they were emphatic support for the general proposition that when enemies fight long enough, they come to resemble each other.

The Polish battlefront was unexpectedly quiet from August 1944 to January 1945. Whereas there was some activity elsewhere, as the Red Army made offensives in the Baltic states and Hungary, here there was a regrouping of armies and a recuperation of divisions. It was believed that once the Germans were fighting on their own soil, they would put up a desperate resistance. At the beginning of 1945 there were two fronts in the north, under Chernyakhovsky (3rd Belorussian) and Rokossovsky (2nd Belorussian), which were to be entrusted with the conquest of East Prussia. In the center Zhukov (1st Belorussian) was waiting to attack Warsaw, after which his men would proceed to Berlin in more or less a straight line. South of Zhukov, Konev's front (1st Ukrainian) was to gain Upper Silesia (which was Hitler's one remaining industrial region). In central Europe, the fronts of Malinovsky, Tolbukhin and Petrov were required to clear the Carpathians and Slovakia, occupy Budapest and then Vienna. The fall of the latter, a vital communications center for

Previous page: Red Army men and an IS-2 heavy tank at the Brandenburg Gate in Berlin.
Below: Soviet infantry employ a flamethrower in house-to-house fighting in Kustrin.

the Germans, was expected to compel a German withdrawal from south east Europe.

The campaign in Hungary had really begun in November, when the Red Army set forth for Budapest from the Plain of Mohacs (where, in 1526, the Ottoman Sultan had assembled his rather smaller army for a similar offensive). By the end of the year Budapest was encircled, but even at this late stage the Germans were able to mount strong counterattacks and although Pest was captured on 18 January it was not until a month later that the Russians were able to grasp Buda, on the other side of the Danube. Vienna was now exposed; a sharp counteroffensive by the Germans around Lake Balaton won a short respite before it petered out for lack of fuel, and on 13 April Vienna was occupied by the Red Army.

What was, and was intended to be, the final grand offensive of the Red Army began on 12 January, when Konev broke out of his Baranov bridgehead with 70 divisions. In two days he covered twenty miles on a quite broad front. On 14 January Zhukov headed out of his two bridgeheads of Magnuszev and Pulawy. With his right wing he passed to the north and west of Warsaw, while with his left he captured Radom. Meanwhile, on 14 January Rokossovsky burst into action against the German defenses covering the southern approach to East Prussia. Hitler, who had directed the Russian campaign from his East Prussian headquarters at Rastenburg, was no longer there, having left for his underground bunker in Berlin. On 15 January the 4th Ukrainian Front moved on Krakow.

Warsaw was completely cut off, and was taken on 17 January. In what was an increasingly frequent sequence, Hitler thereupon found a general for the role of scapegoat and dismissed him. In the first week of the offensive the Red Army had moved about 100 miles closer to Berlin and was taking a quite large number of German prisoners. Loss of Rumanian and Hungarian oil had exacerbated the fuel problem; not only was the Luftwaffe grounded for much of the time but troop withdrawals had to be on foot, making it easy for Soviet motorized formations to

encircle and capture the retreating Germans.

On 20 January Konev was on German soil in Silesia, and two days later he reached the Oder, along which he extended a 60-mile front. In the same week the German Fourth Army broke out of encirclement and withdrew, contrary to Hitler's orders; its commander, and the Army Group North commander (Reinhardt) were thereupon dismissed. Not far away Rokossovsky was moving across into East Prussia. On 20 January he was at Tannenberg, scene of Hindenburg's great victory over the Russians in 1914; before withdrawing the Germans destroyed the commemorative monument there, so as to deny the Russians that pleasure, and also took off with them the remains of Hindenburg and his wife, who had been interred there. When Rokossovsky reached the gulf of Danzig on 26 January he cut off 40 German divisions, which retired on Königsberg.

At first it was thought that Königsberg would be easily captured, but a counterattack by two panzer grenadier divisions, together with the fighting withdrawal, mentioned earlier, of the Fourth Army from Narva, had severely damaged the Russian armies

Top: Czechoslovak units parade through the streets of liberated Prague in 1945.
Above: Red Army troops in action in Vienna in April 1945. Their supporting tank is an American-made Sherman.
Left: SS General Bach-Zelewski who commanded the forces which suppressed the Warsaw Rising with notorious savagery.

Right: The Red Army
helps out in a captured
German town.

Above: A dug-in
Panther tank smashed
by Soviet artillery in
the streets of a German
town. Judging from the
empty shell cases the
tank was involved in
heavy fighting.

there. Rendulic, a commander much favored by Hitler who had been appointed to take over Army Group North from its former disgraced General Reinhardt, was instructed that Königsberg should under no circumstances be given up. As the first sizable German city to be under threat, Hitler believed that Moscow intended to establish there its own new German government, composed of German communists. The Fourth Army, again under a new commander, defended Königsberg with about 23 under-strength divisions. Eight miles away to the west, separated by a strip of Russian-held territory, was the Samland Group of formations amounting to about nine divisions.

After the accumulation of supplies, the Soviet assault on Königsberg began on 13 March. The

Fourth Army's positions were well thought-out and the German resistance was stiff. After six days the German bridgehead still occupied an area twenty miles long and six deep. But Fourth Army was gradually pushed on to the Balga Peninsula, and its morale began to show signs of cracking, with an increasing number of desertions. Hitler refused the request for evacuation by sea, but he changed his mind after a few days, by which time it was too late; some Germans did manage to break out but about 45,000 were captured, together with hundreds of tanks and guns. After this, the final assault on the city could be made. This was achieved with overwhelming force, the German defenders being outnumbered by about four to one. Moreover, by this time the Soviet command had in its service numerous

Germans, sometimes dressed as German soldiers, who could be infiltrated into the city to make attacks or to disrupt services. Koch, by then the Nazi Party boss of East Prussia, had prevented the evacuation of the city's population in accordance with Hitler's orders, but the garrison commander, Lasch, after several days of increasingly hopeless fighting, surrendered. Lasch was then sentenced to death by Hitler *in absentia* and the Red Army soldiers indulged in an orgy of looting, raping and killing among the Königsberg citizens. With the subsequent evacuation by sea of the remnants of the Samland Group, German power in East Prussia was broken, for ever. Königsberg is now in the USSR, and renamed Kaliningrad.

When the Red Army left Soviet territory and advanced into Central Europe there were immediate reports of widespread barbarities and atrocities committed against local populations by its men. These reports soon grew into rumors, often exaggerated, but nevertheless it is undeniable that in some areas unspeakable brutalities were perpetrated, much more than the looting and raping which normally accompanies victorious armies. On the other hand

Left: **One of the last photographs of Hitler, taken in his Berlin bunker in April 1945. In the background a portrait of Frederick the Great whose example in leading Prussia from the brink of catastrophe Hitler hoped to emulate.** *Below:* **The Soviet advance toward Berlin.**

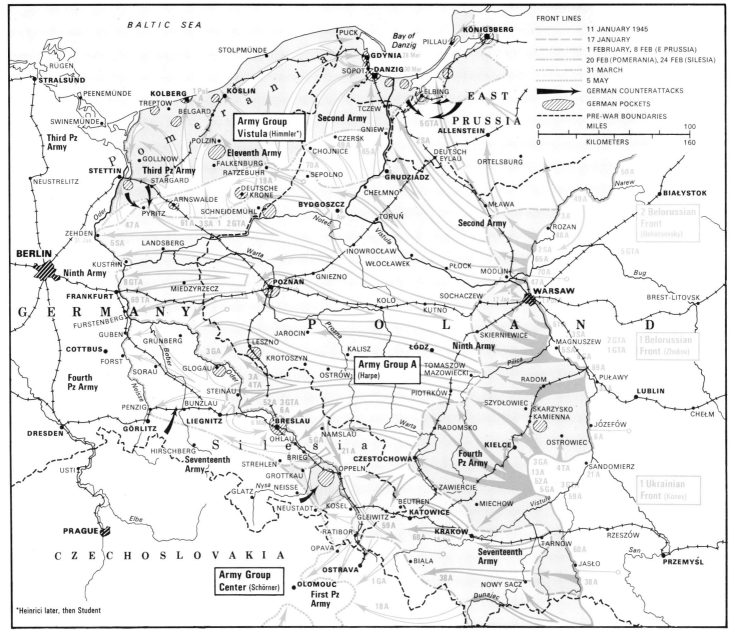

Above: An IS-2 tank leads a Soviet victory parade in Berlin. *Right:* After the capture of Berlin, the first issue of the Soviet-organized newspaper *Berliner Zeitung* is distributed.

Below: A typically devastated Berlin street after the capture of the city.

there were Red Army units which conducted themselves impeccably, and cases where Red Army personnel were severely punished for excesses. That in many instances the Soviet command permitted a relaxation of discipline may be partly ascribable to the hatred with which Germans were regarded by 1945, (although this does not cover bad behavior in non-German parts, even in Tito's Yugoslavia, which had been an ally throughout). From the very beginning of the war Soviet propagandists strove to instil a hatred of Germans among the population, and especially among Red Army men. For example, Simonov, capable of writing good love poems, turned his hand to hate verse, and his poem titled 'Kill Him!' was widely circulated. But in any case, the atrocities committed by Germans in occupied Russia would alone have been sufficient to engender hatred. Moreover, in the course of the war twenty million Russian soldiers and civilians were killed. This was more than one in ten of the Soviet population, which meant that almost every Red soldier and officer had lost a friend or relative by German action. By 1945 self-restraint could hardly be expected.

At the end of January the Russians were within 100 miles of Berlin. But the Germans resisted for another three months, aided by the circumstance that as their area of activity was pushed in, their outnumbered troops were more concentrated. To the extent that Hitler resisted all suggestion that it was time to negotiate, this prolongation of the war may be ascribed to him, but his handling of the military situation actually shortened his army's effective life. His frequent transfers of troops from one front to another, his refusal to permit his troops to withdraw in good time, especially from localities he had designated as fortresses, and his succession of dismissals and appointments, only hampered his commanders. Guderian, who despite his intellectual limitations was now chief of staff, had no chance of pursuing consistent policies so long as Hitler was in overall command. Hitler's emphasis on what he

regarded as 'character' rather than on military talent led him to appoint Himmler as commander of the new Army Group Weichsel [Vistula], set up to stem the Soviet advance from Poland. Himmler had no military talent whatsoever, but fortunately he left the business of running his Army Group to his chief of staff, Wenck, who made the most of his scanty resources.

Hitler had planned to gain a breathing space with his Ardennes offensive in Belgium; by delaying the western allies he would be able to divert some troops to fight the Russians. But the Ardennes operation finally failed, although its abandonment made it possible to send away the Sixth Panzer Army. But contrary to advice, Hitler despatched it not to protect Berlin but to mount his counteroffensives in Hungary. Meanwhile, in late January and early February both Zhukov and Konev crossed the Oder. Zhukov made his crossing near Kustrin, only about 40 miles from Berlin, and by mid-February Konev's front was roughly in line with Zhukov's, having reached the Neisse close to its confluence with the Oder.

Hitler still refused to remove his encircled divisions in Courland, although German naval preponderance in the Baltic would have made this an easy operation; he said that the more or less inactive German troops there were holding down large numbers of Red divisions. This was hardly true, because the Russians were still by-passing enemy strongpoints in favor of a speedy advance; Zhukov, advancing over the Polish plains, had by-passed Breslau in this way. So in mid-February when Guderian began a desperate counteroffensive he had to rely mainly on Wenck's troops. Wenck himself, however, after an interview with Hitler, fell asleep at the wheel of his car when driving back to his headquarters, and was seriously injured. He was succeeded by Krebs, who lacked Wenck's flair. Even worse, at this point Himmler decided to take a closer interest in decisions, which meant that the offensive petered out. It had, however, forced the

Red Army to abandon the possibility of an assault on Berlin as early as February, before it secured its position on the east side of the Oder. Towards the end of February, however, Rokossovsky scored successes against the ammunition-starved panzer armies in Pomerania. Zhukov joined in, and eventually the panzers were forced out of the region, mostly evacuating by sea. Konev, meantime, consolidated his previous advances by broadening his

Left: A German soldier surveys the end of the Reich.
Bottom left: The Soviet flag is planted on the Reichstag.
Below: Keitel signs the surrender document in Berlin, signifying Germany's final defeat.

they knocked out scores of Soviet tanks in the streets of Berlin. Other contributions to the defense of Berlin came from Luftwaffe detachments, the Hitler Youth organization, armed police, and supply and service troops.

The final assault began on 16 April, by which time Army Group Vistula, to which the defense was committed, was commanded by Heinrici. Three fronts were to undertake the Russian drive; Rokossovsky's 2nd Belorussian Front began four days after Zhukov's and Kovev's even though it had to move the greater distance, from East Prussia and Pomerania. Zhukov, perhaps because of his closer relationship with Stalin, had been given the prized shortest line of attack. In any case he was in overall command of the operation and left the control of his 1st Belorussian Front to Sokolovsky. Konev was required to direct the bulk of his forces to Dresden and Prague.

On the first day the 1st Belorussian Front was held by the quite strong German defense lines, but Konev managed to progress just six miles, and soon after had crossed the Spree, Berlin's own river. On Hitler's birthday, 20 April, the situation was that Konev's Third and Fourth Guards Tank Armies had broken through and were only 10 miles from Zossen, the location of OKW, while Rokossovsky's 2nd Belorussian Front was on the move over the lower Oder, and the 1st Belorussian Front, while held up at its center, had managed to send the 2nd Guards Tank Army round the flank on to an autobahn ten miles north of the capital. The German Ninth Army's commander, Busse, requested Hitler's permission to withdraw from the Oder to protect his rear; Hitler refused. Meanwhile the Führer had launched a counterattack by his Fourth Panzer Army; this made some progress but the operation petered out when it was discovered that the promised supporting units hardly existed except on paper.

By the following day three Guards tank armies had reached the outer defense ring at various parts of Berlin's outskirts, while the Eighth Guards Army was also active. By 25 April Berlin had been encircled and, further south, the American and Soviet armies made contact at Torgau, on the Elbe. Rokossovsky was some way from Berlin, but opened the way by breaking through the Third Panzer Army south of Stettin. Still, apparently, confident, Hitler planned a series of counterattacks with his remaining forces on 25 April. At first, reports of their progress seemed to elate Hitler but by 27 April it was clear that they had been blocked. The Red Army was well into the city from several directions, being resisted by a parachute division, a panzer division composed of trainees and instructors, some odd panzer units and a French SS unit. On 30 April the Reichstag was captured and the Red Army was barely a thousand yards from Hitler's bunker. Hitler committed suicide, with some of his associates, and on 2 May the city surrendered. For a few more days Admiral Dönitz was in charge. He had been named by Hitler as his successor, because the Führer no longer trusted men like Göring and Himmler, whom he rightly suspected of seeking negotiations. Then, on 7 May, Jodl signed an unconditional surrender document presented by the Anglo-Americans. Two days later Keitel signed a second such document in the presence of Soviet representatives in Berlin.

Above: Stalin, with Molotov on his right, at the Potsdam Conference in early August 1945, which was intended to settle the fate of Germany. The newly elected British Prime Minister Attlee (bald with glasses) is at the extreme left. A youthful Gromyko faces the camera at the extreme right.

front on the Neisse. While all this was going on the Second and Sixth Panzer armies were mounting a counteroffensive in Hungary, aided by unenthusiastic Hungarian units. Their progress was very slow and, after the Hungarians collapsed, the armored formations were badly mauled.

The final stage of the war was the so-called race to Berlin. There was a race, but it was not between the Russians and the western allies, for the Americans had no plans to make a dash for Berlin. Rather was the race between Konev and Zhukov, who both displayed an unseemly jealousy in this matter, each intent on winning the honor of capturing the German capital and, if possible, Adolf Hitler himself. The German army was now largely composed of *Volkssturm* units. These had begun to appear in 1944, and consisted of men between the ages of 16 and 60, called up from civilian life and, for the most part, not provided with proper uniforms. They were organized by the local Nazi political heads, *Gauleiters*, and therefore formed part of neither the Wehrmacht nor the SS, but were a Nazi party creation. Some fought enthusiastically, while others did not. In conventional mobile warfare they were of little use, but in local engagements on their home soil they were often surprisingly effective. Armed with the hollow-charge antitank rocket projector (Panzerfaust), and often carrying these weapons around on their bicycles,

Below: The celebrated meeting on the Elbe of the advanced Russian and US units.

INDEX

FURTHER READING

Over two hundred substantial books have been published about this war, mainly in Russian or German. Of these, a handful have been translated. Of those available in English, many are by participants, typically Soviet or German generals, part of whose purpose in writing is to explain or defend themselves (usually by shifting blame on to other shoulders). Among the participants whose memoirs have been translated are, on the German side, Guderian (*Panzer Leader*, 1952), Halder (*Hitler as War Lord*, 1950), Keitel (*Memoirs*, 1965), and Manstein (*Lost Victories*, 1958). From the Soviet side, there are English-language editions of memoirs by Chuikov (*The Beginning of the Road*, 1963, and *The End of the Third Reich*, 1967), Golovko (*With the Red Fleet*, 1965), and Zhukov (*Memoirs*, 1969).

However, it is more rewarding to read the several scholarly syntheses which have recently become available. These tend to be more objective and, because they draw on all the available sources, both wider-ranging and deeper. They also provide long bibliographies. Eminent among them are the books of J. Erickson (*The Soviet High Command 1918–1941*, 1962, *The Road to Stalingrad*, 1975, *The Road to Berlin*, 1984) and Albert Seaton (*The Russo-German War 1941–1945*, 1971, and *Stalin as Warlord*, 1976).

Also of use are James F. Dunnigan (Editor): *The Russian Front*, 1978, which is strong on weaponry and orders of battle, and Barry H. Leach's scholarly *German Strategy against Russia 1939–1941*, 1973.

ACKNOWLEDGMENTS

The author and publishers would like to thank Design 23 who designed this book and Ron Watson who compiled the index. The following agencies kindly supplied the illustrations.
BISON PICTURE LIBRARY: pp 6–7, 10 lower right, 14 top, 14–15, 15 both, 18–19 all four, 22–23 all three, 25 bottom, 27 left, 30–31 all three, 90, 102 bottom, 103, 106, 107 bottom, 110 top, 111, 118, 121, 122 top, 124 top, 126 bottom, 127 top, 187
BUNDESARCHIV: pp 24 top, 28 top left, 40, 44, 64, 84 bottom, 100 upper, 110 center, 143 top, 165 bottom, 172 bottom, 176 top
BUNDESARCHIV (via RHL): pp 14 bottom, 21 lower, 26, 35, 36–37, 41, 42, 48–49, 52–53, 54, 55 both, 61 top, 70–71, 72–73, 82 lower left, 82–83, 83 top, 84 upper, 86–87 both, 88 bottom, 101 center, 104 bottom, 105 center & bottom, 118 top, 124 bottom, 147 top, 148, 160 top, 164 bottom
FOX PHOTOS: p 13 lower
ROBER HUNT LIBRARY: pp 2–3, 8, 9, 11, 27 right, 46, 49, 51 both inset, 59, 60–61, 66–67, 68, 69 both, 84 lower, 88 center, 89 bottom, 98–99, 101 top & bottom, 104 top, 112 bottom, 119, 123 both, 128 right, 129, 142, 145 center, 147 bottom left, 149 both, 162–163, 165 top, 170 center, 185 bottom
IMPERIAL WAR MUSEUM, London (via RHL): pp 20 bottom, 38, 151 top, 156 bottom
NATIONAL ARCHIVES (US): p 12 lower
MAPS © Richard Natkiel: pp 10, 39, 56, 102, 144, 166, 174, 187
NOVOSTI: pp 1, 4–5, 10 upper right, 12 upper, 13 top, 16–17, 20 top, 21 upper, 24 lower two, 25 top, 28 center left, 28–29, 32–33 all five, 34 both, 43, 45, 47, 50–51 main pic, 57, 58, 62–63, 65, 74–75, 76, 77, 78–79, 80, 81 both, 82 top left, 84 top, 88 top, 89 top, 91, 92–93 both, 94 all three, 95, 96 both, 97, 100 lower, 104 upper & center left, 105 top, 107 top, 108–109 all six, 110 bottom, 112 top, 113 all three, 114–115, 116 top, 116–117, 120, 120–121, 122 bottom, 125 both, 126 upper, 127 bottom, 128 both left, 132–133 both, 134–135 all four, 136–137 both, 138–139, 140–141, 143 center & bottom, 145 top & bottom, 146 all four, 147 bottom right, 150, 151 bottom, 152, 153, 154 both, 155, 156 top, 157 both, 158–159, 160 bottom, 161, 164 upper, 165 center, 167 top & bottom, 168, 169, 170 top & bottom, 171, 172 top, 173 both, 174–175, 176 center & bottom, 177, 179 both, 180, 181 both, 182–183, 184, 185 center & top, 186 both, 188–189 all six, 190 both
NOVOSTI (via RHL): 167 center, 178